"Just superb. . . . Funny, too. . . . Talmud, Torah, Jack Lemmon,
Bill Murray—need I say more?" —Mark Oppenheimer, author of
THIRTEEN AND A DAY: THE BAR AND BAT MITZVAH ACROSS AMERICA

Be a *mensh* and check out
Michael Wex's other books.

T here are people out there,
millions of them, who act as if they still believe
everything their mothers told them in the
first six months of their life—that they're the
nicest, most beautiful, and most promising
and intelligent bags of flesh ever to walk the
[ea]rth. . . . these people *shmucks*.

. . . *Be a Mensh (and Not a
. . . -selling* author Michael Wex
offers a wise and witty guide to being a good
human being, regardless of your religion
or beliefs. Referencing pop culture, current
events, and Jewish tradition with equal ease,
Wex explores the strategies developed by an
oppressed people to pursue happiness with
their dignity—and sense of humor—intact.

_____

Novelist, lecturer, and translator MICHAEL WEX
is one of the leading lights in the revival of
Yiddish, and author of the *New York Times*
bestseller *Born to Kvetch* and its follow-up,
Just Say Nu.

www.michaelwex.com

Praise for
Michael Wex
and
How to Be a Mentsh (and Not a Shmuck)

"Funny. . . . Astute and relevant." —*San Francisco Chronicle*

"Blessed with humor, grace, and a well-developed sense of contemporary pop culture—references range from Genesis to *Groundhog Day*. . . . A consistent pleasure: entertaining, educational . . . with more than a few thought-provoking suggestions for achieving *mentsh*-hood—or at least avoiding *shmuck*-itude." —*Publishers Weekly* (starred review)

"The Sneaky Chef of contemporary Jewish culture . . . Wex writes books that look and read like snacks, but he hides scholarly vegetables between the covers. . . . Wex has achieved on the bookshelf what Hillel advised that we all do in life: In a place where there are no *mentshn*, try to be a *mentsh*."
—*Forward*

"An often humorous and frequently provocative guide to being a good person, a *mentsh*. . . . This book reflects extensive learning, serious thought, a sense of the absurd and the unfair, as well as an impish willingness to play the *mazik* (scamp)."
—*Jewish Book World*

"I know it's a vain hope, but when I grow up I want to be Michael Wex."
—Theodore Bikel, musician and Academy Award nominee

How to Be a Mentsh

(and Not a Shmuck)

How to Be a Mentsh
(and Not a Shmuck)

Michael Wex

HARPER ⬤ PERENNIAL

NEW YORK • LONDON • TORONTO • SYDNEY • NEW DELHI • AUCKLAND

HARPER ● PERENNIAL

A hardcover edition of this book was published in 2009 by Harper-Collins Publishers.

P.S.™ is a trademark of HarperCollins Publishers.

HarperCollins books may be purchased for educational, business, or sales promotional use. For information please write: Special Markets Department, HarperCollins Publishers, 10 East 53rd Street, New York, NY 10022.

FIRST HARPER PERENNIAL EDITION PUBLISHED 2010.

Designed by Cassandra J. Pappas

The Library of Congress has catalogued the hardcover edition as follows:
Wex, Michael.
   How to be a mentsh (and not a shmuck) / Michael Wex.—1st ed.
     p. cm.
   Includes bibliographical references and index.
   ISBN 978-0-06-177111-8
  1. Yiddish language—Terms and phrases. 2. Yiddish language—Idioms. 3. Yiddish language—Social aspects. 4. Yiddish wit and humor. I. Title.
   PJ5113.W483 2009
   181'.060207—dc22   2009010476

ISBN 978-0-06-177112-5 (pbk.)

10 11 12 13 14   OV/RRD   10 9 8 7 6 5 4 3 2 1

In memory of my mother

Acknowledgments

Had Leigh Haber not suggested that I write something about how to be a *mentsh*, the subject would never have occurred to me. Had Bob Bookman and I not been talking about Billy Wilder one day, I might never have figured out how I wanted to write it. Had my parents not taught me to shut up and listen when smart people are talking, I might have missed both opportunities.

I'd also like to thank Betsy Rapoport for connecting me with my agent, Richard Pine, a real *mentsh*, without whose advocacy and advice this book would have remained nothing more than an idea. Stephanie Meyers, my editor at Harper, has been a pleasure to work with at every stage of this project. Her attention to detail and sympathetic approach to occasionally gnarly material meshed perfectly with the contents of the book.

Without these *mentshn*, this book would not exist.

Without my wife, Marilla, and my daughter, Sabina, the same could probably be said for me.

Contents

A Note on Spelling and Terminology, with a Prologue to Any Further Kvetching

I

MANY PEOPLE READING this sentence have already looked at the cover of this book and snorted derisively. *"Ach, du lieber! I knew it all along. The kvetch-guy, the big expert, the Grand Poobah of Yiddish, should give Dan Quayle a call and ask for lessons in spelling. Mentsh, my eye. Everyone knows that the word is spelled mensch."*

And if we were all speaking German today, it would be. A bagel and schmeer would be spelled *Begel und Schmier*, *lox* would be *Lachs*, and we'd think of all three as wholesome Teutonic delicacies straight from the *Vaterland*—because a *Mensch*, one of a certain age, at least, would be a solid citizen whose service in the *Wehrmacht* or on the home front had helped Germany conquer the world. The kind of *mentsh* described in this book would probably be a thing of the past; and I, were I lucky enough to be alive, might have written a book—as underground as any bestseller can be—about a language that was born to *quetsch*.

Let's not belabor the obvious, then: Yiddish and German are two separate and very different languages that use different alphabets and reflect wholly different ways of thinking. If you're worried about what *mentsh* is *really* supposed to look like, imagine a cover that reads:

How to Be a מענטש *and Not a* שמאָק

The authentic Yiddish *mentsh* has no truck with any ABCs. The best we can try to do is come up with a substitute as close to the original in sound and meaning as possible. Unlike the German *Mensch*, the Yiddish *mentsh* has a definite *t*-sound between the *n* and the *sh*; unlike the German, it isn't German, though it could certainly be described as Germanic. The Yiddish *mentsh* sounds no more like *Mensch* than the German *ist* sounds like the English *is*. Where *is* and *ist* mean the same thing, though, we'll see over the course of this book that the Yiddish *mentsh* differs from *Mensch* even more in meaning than in spelling or pronunciation.

The Latin-alphabet *mentsh* is also an internationalism, the transliteration sanctioned by YIVO, the Académie Française of the Yiddish-speaking world, for use in all languages that employ the Latin alphabet. To use *Mensch* in its stead is to deny Yiddish-speakers the right to ensure that their language is represented with a maximum of accuracy in other languages. *Mentsh* was even used instead of *Mensch* in Yiddish transliterated in Germany before World War II, and people who can get their heads around the idea that *Beijing* renders the name of the Chinese capital more accurately than *Peking* shouldn't have any problem with *mentsh*.

The second Yiddish word in the title presents no such trouble; it isn't really German at all and has nothing to with the German *Schmuck*, which means "jewelry." While Yiddishists might have preferred to see *shmuk* instead of *shmuck*, I felt in this instance that the latter spelling came closer to satisfying everybody—my favorite way of satisfying nobody (see pages 36–37)—especially because *shmuck* is used a bit differently in this book from the way it is used in Yiddish. Although *mentsh* can be used of both men and women in Yiddish, the Yiddish *shmuck* applies only to males. On the basis of the same principle that allows *etiquette*, the French for "label" or "price tag," to mean nothing but "good manners" in English, I have extended the reach of *shmuck* in English to cover people of either sex who don't know how to behave. One need only compare the French *con*—a "c-word" that also means jerk of either sex—to see the same principle at work on the other side of the anatomical divide.

In the same spirit, *shmek*, the correct Yiddish plural of *shmuck*, is used interchangeably with *shmucks*, a highly anglicized version of the same idea.

II

SOME TERMS THAT come up fairly often in the book might not be immediately familiar to people who have not attended a Jewish day school. The Talmud, for instance, consists of two sections. The earlier one, completed around 200 C.E., is called the Mishna. The Mishna was compiled in Hebrew and consists, for the most part, of attempts to organize and interpret the practical applications of the Bible's commandments. The part known as either the Gemara or the Talmud (the latter name has come to be used for the whole collection) was finished about three hundred years after the Mishna. It is mostly in Aramaic and consists, loosely speaking, of commentary on the Mishna. There are two different Talmuds, compiled in two different places and containing much divergent material. These are commonly known as the Babylonian and Jerusalem Talmuds. Historically, the Babylonian has been the more important. In the few citations to the Jerusalem Talmud in this text, the word *Yerushalmi* precedes the name of the tractate from which the quotation has been drawn.

The Talmud became essential to Judaism after the destruction of the Second Temple in 70 C.E. The destruction of the Temple and the accompanying loss of Jewish political autonomy mark the beginning of Judaism as we know it, a religion characterized by exile and dislocation. Until the year 70, Jewish practice revolved around offering sacrifices at the Temple in Jerusalem. The Talmud and its way of thinking helped to change a religion focused on a specific location into one that can be taken anywhere with no loss of intensity or authenticity. As I have written elsewhere, "Acceptance of Talmudic authority marks the real difference between Jews and the rest of the world."

Midrash is a collective designation for various types of homiletic interpretation of the Bible. Although the main midrashic collections were compiled during the Middle Ages, the material contained in these collections is often of considerably greater antiquity.

Rashi is the acronym by which Rabbi *Sh*lomo *Y*itskhoki (died 1104) is known. He is the author of the best-known and most influential commentaries on both the Bible and Talmud, commentaries that are printed alongside the text of both works and studied as a virtual part of them in traditional religious schools.

The *Shulkhan Arukh* ("The Set Table") is the title of a legal code by Rabbi Joseph Karo (died 1545) that has become authoritative for Orthodox Jews of every stripe. It serves as the basic rule book of halacha, as Jewish law is called in Hebrew.

Unless otherwise noted, all translations are my own.

Introduction:

Don't Be a Shmuck

THIS IS A book about happiness, your own and that of others. It's a book about living decently without preaching about it or turning into a Goody Two-shoes like Ned Flanders on *The Simpsons*. It is based on an idea of what it means to be fully human, an idea developed by people who have been labeled as subhuman on more than one occasion. It's about how to care for yourself by thinking about others.

It doesn't matter who you are, where you come from, what religion you follow, or if you follow any religion at all. The principles outlined in this book will work for anyone who makes the effort to put them into practice, and as we'll see, the most important one of all originates in a piece of advice that a rabbi gave to a gentile. Although some of the explanations of Jewish tradition that follow might sound a little esoteric or out of the way, they're here to show how theory was turned into practice. I first learned the basic ideas treated here at home and heard most of them from my mother, who didn't know one page of

Talmud from the next, but had pretty clear ideas about what it means to be a *mentsh*. The same ideas, often expressed in the form of proverbs, have also been passed down by millions of other Jewish mothers over the course of many centuries.

The saying that I probably heard most often was, "It's never too late to die or to get married." My mother, who lived to be forty-eight, didn't have much to say about dying, but getting married was a whole other matter. How is getting married like dying? It happens every day, she would explain, but isn't as easy as it looks. If you do it right, getting married means deliberately putting yourself into a position in which it becomes impossible for you to think of yourself as the center of your world, as more important than somebody else, ever again. As far as she and millions of other Jewish parents across the generations were concerned, getting married is a kind of shorthand for growing up and assuming responsibility, for voluntarily relinquishing the comfortable but ultimately sterile self-absorption that only children, who don't have to look out for themselves, and the single, who look out for nobody *but* themselves, can really afford to maintain. As the movie version of Neil Simon's *Come Blow Your Horn* has it:

LEE J. COBB: You're a bum.

FRANK SINATRA: Why am I a bum, Dad?

LJC: Are you married?

FS: No.

LJC: Then you're a bum.

This is why the Yiddish-speaking world refers to unmarried men and women, no matter how old they might be, by terms that also mean "adolescent" or "youth"—someone not quite grown-up. They might have matured physically, but they haven't taken the final step into maturity: they're bums.

When a Yiddish-speaker says that it's never too late to get married, they're saying that it's never too late to learn that the only thing that's really special about you is the ability to set your own self aside once in a while, to make somebody else more special than you are. "It's never too late to get married" means that it's never too late to learn consideration, the art of thinking about others because they're worthy of being thought about. If it's never too late, you've always got a chance to wise up and become a *mentsh*, whether you actually get married or not.

Of course, the longer you leave it, the harder it gets and the less likely it becomes. That's where becoming a *mentsh* differs from dropping dead. There are people out there, millions of them, who act as if they still believe everything that their mothers told them in the first six months of their lives: they're the nicest, most beautiful, most promising and intelligent bags of flesh ever to walk the earth, and anybody who can't see it is foolish or wicked—and certainly jealous. Who could dislike someone to whom Jesus himself would have been sending daily Facebook friend-requests, had his Father in Heaven only hearkened to his pleas to be born a couple of millennia later, just so Mary could get him a laptop for Chanukah (since Christmas wouldn't be such a big thing yet), and lonesome baby Jesus could log on and find that one special person whom he knows, really *knows* to be the real thing—the smartest, nicest, most beautiful and talented of all his little sunbeams—and ask to be their Facebook pal, and when they finally pay attention and answer and write on his wall, let's just say that Jesus learns the meaning of Xmas at last.

There are people, lots of people, who act as if they're Jesus's Christmas present and resent anyone who dares to disagree. You don't have to look too far to find them. The number of people and institutions destroyed by Bernard Madoff gets bigger by the day; the economy has tanked as a result of unrestrained greed on Wall Street and an unrestrained desire on Main Street to get something—especially a house—for what looked to a sap like nothing.

Rod Blagojevich, the Illinois governor whose attempt to sell Barack Obama's Senate seat is being reported on the radio as I write this paragraph, is practically a poster boy for the attitude that I'm trying to describe. "I've got this thing," he said—the FBI has him on tape—"and it's fucking golden. And, uh, uh, I'm just not giving it up for fuckin' nothing. I'm not going to do it."

Governor Blagojevich is just following the advice of so many "be as rich as you want" gurus. He's thinking outside the usual governmental envelope, and is hardly the only guy in contemporary America who's trying to monetize the resources at his disposal. The merchandise might not be typical, but his attitude is hardly unusual: as a society, as a culture, we seem to have lost sight of the difference between getting our due and getting our way. At one level or another, whether it's got to do with basic manners, corporate greed, or good old-fashioned political corruption, this confusion seems to lie at the root of the all too common "because I could" justification for harmful and stupid things popularized by Bill Clinton.

"Because I could" is "fuck you" in disguise. We might think

that we're self-actualizing, when we are really self-centered and mean, with so powerful a sense of entitlement to whatever we think should be ours—whether it's something we already have or something we want—that there's no room for anyone to get in our way. We want it, we're going to get it; and if it's at someone else's expense, who cares? Just as long as they're somebody else. We've been in a moral coma for too long now, one that sounds as if it could have been inspired by the old vernacular translation of *per ardua ad astra*, the motto of the Royal Canadian Air Force. The Latin means "through hardships to the stars," but the whole country knew that it *really* meant, "Fuck you, Jack, I'm fireproof."

"Consequences are for other people." Anybody might have said so; a *shmuck* is someone who really believes it, and usually does so unconsciously.

This is a book about how to keep yourself from believing that you're somebody special. It's about how not to be a *shmuck*.

How to Be a Mentsh

(and Not a Shmuck)

ONE

What's a *Shmuck?*

I

My MOTHER NEVER told me anything about *shmek*, as more than one *shmuck* is called in Yiddish. She never uttered the word in my presence, not in English and certainly not in Yiddish, and might never have said it in her life. It wouldn't have been ladylike; it wouldn't even have been polite. Although most people who speak English are now familiar with the word, those who don't know any Yiddish are often unaware of its literal meaning. English has borrowed *shmuck*'s extended meanings of "jerk, fool, metaphorical asshole and inconsiderate idiot who has no idea of the effect that he has on others" directly from Yiddish, but has left the original meaning, the one that generated all these other associations, so far behind that English-speakers are often shocked to discover that *shmuck* is one of the "dirtiest" words in Yiddish, the sort of thing that could make your mother try to wash your mouth out with soap, even if you're fifty years old when you say it. If you think of the power that *fuck* used to have in polite conversation, how it could convey both emphasis *and* offense, you'll have some idea of the force that *shmuck* still retains in Yiddish.

Its primary meaning in Yiddish is "penis," but just as *prick, dick, pecker, whang,* and *pork-sword* frequently reach beyond simple anatomy and into the realm of character analysis, so does *shmuck.* Unlike any of these English terms, though, or even such straightforward designations as *tallywhacker* or *man-meat, shmuck* started out as something cute and funny rather than big and potentially bothersome. It has its roots in the nursery, in little boys' discovery of themselves and the world around them, and began not as *shmuck,* the dirty word, but as *shmekele*—"shmucklet"—something much smaller than a *shmuck,* not as fully developed, and much more socially acceptable; a peashooter instead of a pistol.

Shmekele itself seems to have started out as *shtekele,* "little stick," the euphemism used by toddlers and their baby-talking parents for a little boy's penis. *Shtekele* is a diminutive form of the now obsolete *shtok,* which means "stick" or "club," and must also have referred to a full-grown male member (compare the difference between a big, thick cigar and its diminutive, cigarette); if a *shtok* is a walking stick, the *shtekl,* in this usage, becomes something of a candy cane.

It isn't entirely a matter of size, though. Somebody must have noticed that the little stick wasn't always as rigid as a stick is supposed to be—technically speaking, only the infantile erection is a *shtekele*—so the well-known *shm* prefix was substituted for the first few consonants, as if to say, "*Shtekele, shmekele*! Just look at it now. We know it's not really a cute little stick, so why don't we call it a *shmute little shmick.*"

The *shm* prefix is one of the great Yiddish contributions to the English language. It can take anything, no matter how frightening, and make it innocuous, unthreatening, unimportant—quite a significant trick for victims of constant persecution. If you can't defeat an enemy or deal with a threat, the least you can do is to turn it into a joke:

MR. COHEN: Hello, Mr. Levy. How's your wife these days?

MR. LEVY: *Freg nisht*, don't ask. She was just diagnosed with cancer.

MR. COHEN: Cancer, shmancer, *abi gezunt*, as long as she's healthy.

This surprisingly popular old joke is still circulating in many versions, all of which turn on the reaction of Cohen, a know-it-all who isn't really listening and doesn't really care about the welfare of Levy's wife. He is so quick to throw in a *shm* in order to cut Levy's troubles down to their proper size—smaller than Cohen's, no matter how big they might look to Levy—so quick to come out with the standard kvetch-squelcher *abi gezunt*, "as long as you're healthy," that he misses the all too painful fact that this time it's something serious.

There's nothing wrong with saying "cancer, shmancer," if what comes next is "I'm going to beat it" or "We just found a cure." Take away Cohen and his self-regard, and the *shm* helps to diminish the disease, rather than the sufferer, and show it who's boss: the comedienne Fran Drescher, a survivor of uterine cancer, has written a book called *Cancer Schmancer* (that's her spelling, not mine) and founded an organization with the same name dedicated to ensuring "that all women with cancer are diagnosed in stage 1, when it is most curable"; to turning cancer, in other words, into shmancer, something that might once have been important but isn't anymore. The most it can do is pretend to a status that we all know it doesn't have, in the same way as someone or something that you label as "fancy-shmancy" is not really so fancy after all: the *shm* explodes the pretensions of the thing, action, or quality that it modifies and then does its best to scorn these things into nothingness.

In its attempt to make such things disappear, *shm* can also let you know that only a fool, an out-and-out unreconstructed idiot, could really think that the thing in question is worth talking about. It's a distraction, a red herring—the only herring that Yiddish does not take seriously—something that has obtruded itself into a place where it shouldn't be:

MRS. COHEN: So, tell me, Mrs. Levy, when's your
    granddaughter getting married?
MRS. LEVY: Married, shmarried! She's nine months old.

"Don't," in other words, "be stupid. Where does marriage come to toilet training? If you can't be bothered to start making sense, the least you could do is make sure not to talk."

The path from *shtekele* to *shmekele*, from *sht* to *shm*, leads from childish whimsy to childish knowingness: regardless of what adults might think, kids can not only tell the difference between image and reality, they can also figure out which parts of their bodies will make grown-ups wrinkle their noses as much as the pee-pee and poo-poo that come out of those parts.

They are learning to use these parts for comic effect, especially those of little boys, who have something that they can point and wave solely for the sake of fun.

Now, *shmekele*, the-little-stick-that-isn't, is what linguists call a second-degree diminutive. If Mike is the first-degree diminutive of Michael, Mikey, the diminutive of Mike, is a second-degree diminutive. If *shmekele* is a second-degree diminutive, there should also be a first-degree form, maybe a bit more serious but no whit less cutesy. *Shmekl*, the first-degree diminutive, does in fact exist, and is nearly as common in Yiddish as its little brother, *shmekele*. What's unusual, though, is that there was no positive form, no base-word on which the diminutives depended. A *shmekele* was never really a diminutive *shmok* (the standard Yiddish form of *shmuck*); a *shmok* was an overgrown *shmekele*. Where the linguistic process of whittling a stick down to size begins with the full-sized *shtok*, which becomes a *shtekl* and then a *shtekele*, the more strictly penile progression, marked by the *shm* at the beginning, also works like the real thing: it starts off with something small, then teases it out to fullness.

Shmekl is not the only Yiddish word that contempt has made big. The word *sheytl*, which means the wig worn by Orthodox women to hide their own hair, looks and sounds like a diminutive, even though it really is not. Unable to find a full-sized form in the language as they knew it, though, Yiddish-speakers invented one: the *shoyt* is a larger, hairier, more mature version of the *sheytl*. Since anyone who's spent much time in the Orthodox world can spot even a good *sheytl* from a hundred yards off—they're not *supposed* to look too much like a woman's real hair—it isn't surprising that *shoyt* is used only to refer to a *sheytl* that's less fashionable, more obviously fake, much easier to spot at a distance than the average *sheytl*. When the diminutive is also the norm, the *shoyt*, which becomes monstrous by virtue of its size, is a sign of something gone grotesquely wrong.

If enlarging a diminutive can turn a ladies' toupee into a hunting trophy, imagine what it can do for something that can grow on its own. *Shmok* is to *shmekl* as *shoyt* is to *sheytl*—the only difference being that *sheytl* was always a "real" word, while *shmekl* was invented to make fun of *shtekl* and originally made no real sense without it, any more than a statement that we'd got just got back from Lost Wages would make sense to anyone who had never heard of Las Vegas. We're dealing with a mocking deformation of *shtekele* that grows into an equally sardonic takeoff of the full-sized *shtok* from which the *shtekele* grew.

Fabricating a positive form out of a humorous, baby-talk diminutive is no laughing matter; the full-sized *shmok* is to the child's *shmekl* as the giant ants that try to destroy Los Angeles in the 1954 classic *Them* are to the little fellows that King Solomon tells us to emulate. "Go to the ant, o slacker," he says in Proverbs 6:6, "behold her ways and wise up." Go to any ant in this movie, though, and it'll eat you alive while Edmund Gwenn (Santa Claus in the original *Miracle on 34th Street*) stands helplessly by and watches. What's cute and instructive and ecologically helpful when it's half an inch long is entirely different when it grows to nine feet.

A *shmekele* is small and cute and can sometimes be very funny. Its owner might wave it around once in a while, and the absolute worst it can do is to give the owner himself and anyone in the line of fire a good soaking. With respect to Jewish life, it's the only visible sign that a child too young to wear a yarmulke or ritual fringes is in fact a Jew. "Small is beautiful" comes to an end at roughly the same time as the *shmekele*, grown considerably larger, becomes capable of more than what Chaucer called "purgacioun of uryne." By the time we get to *shmok*, the *shm* is simply the first part of the word, as it is in such other well-known Yiddish terms as *shmatte* or *shmooz*, in which the *shm* has no connection with the pejorative prefix. *Shmok* becomes a word like any other, only dirtier. Technically speaking, *shmok* masquerades as the full-sized, positive form from which the diminutives *shmekl* and *shmekele* are derived: compare a boy four or five years old who goes up to the lady next door and announces proudly, "I have a penis," to a man of thirty who does the same thing. That's the difference between a *shmekl* and a *shmok*.

II

As BOTH THE ant and the penis teach us, enlarging a diminutive, blowing it up as if life and speech were photo labs, can turn something that used to be cute into something unpleasant and often frightening. Growth alone, though, doesn't account for the aura of really distasteful obscenity that still clings to *shmuck* in Yiddish. Where such English terms as *prick* and *dick* can hardly be called sophisticated, using them in polite company to refer to either a penis or a person will cause real offense only if the person, his penis, or some of his friends and family are present. The speaker's breeding, education, and social skills might be called into question; his choice of words might be labeled inappropriate, but not as overtly offensive as *asshole* or worse, *cunt*, would have been in the same conversation. *Shmuck*'s power to offend derives from its deeper cultural context, from a couple of unusual features of Jewish religious and cultural life.

The most significant of these is the central importance of circumcision in Jewish life. As the only ritual that the religion itself considers indispensable—the word *orel*, "man with a foreskin," is a synonym for gentile in both Hebrew and Yiddish—circumcision was until recently considered the infallible sign of the Jew throughout Europe and the Americas. This identification of circumcision with Judaism, the idea that a man's penis can determine the nature of his relationship with God, invests the child's *shmekl* with a significance and allure that might not be immediately apparent to adherents of other faiths. It's not unusual for a Yiddish-speaking mother to lift up the baby boy whom she's diapering and, while cataloging the rest of his body parts and their beauty, wax just as dithyrambic over what she will inevitably call his *kosher shmekele*, his kosher little *shmekl*, the one body part that, even for the baby's mother, has more to do with Mount Sinai than with cocktail weenies, no matter how strictly kosher the latter.

An equally powerful tradition, the role of which is slightly less easy to discern at first glance, is the Jewish refusal—strictly speaking, the Jewish inability—to utter the Tetragrammaton, the four-letter name of God that is said to be His only real name. It's what God calls Himself when He's at home. So powerful is the prohibition against saying it—when the Temple was still standing, no one but the High Priest was allowed to utter it, and even he could do so only on Yom Kippur—that the secret of its pronunciation was lost after the Temple was destroyed:

you couldn't say it if you wanted to. Another, less sacred name is used in its place, one that everybody knows is a less powerful substitute. God's real name can be seen in any Torah, but it is never heard; anything you can call Him involves some kind of diminution. The prohibition against using God's name has expanded to the point where the stand-ins have acquired a taboo quality of their own, as have even some of the substitutes for the substitutes. You'll say *adonai* when praying, but *adoshem* or *Ha-Shem* (literally, The Name) when merely making reference to God. You'll say *elohim* in prayer, but otherwise it's *elokim*: what would look like blasphemy anywhere else—imagine calling Jesus, Mesus—is a sign of respect among Jews.

Although Yiddish has more than its share of euphemism and antiphrasis—calling a fat person Tiny or an evil eye a good eye—the only things or beings whose names are programmatically excluded from a child's universe are God and the kid's own penis. No living being, young or old, knows what God is really called, and no little boy knows the real name of his *shtekl* or *shmekl*. All he knows about it is that his penis is no *shtekele*, no candy cane, and that it is the only part of his body that doesn't seem to have a name of its own. *Shmekl* thus expresses an *attitude* to *shtekl*, a name that the child quickly learns has nothing to do with the part of him to which it's supposed to refer. An arm is an arm; a leg, a leg; even his *tukhes*, or rear end, has a name that it doesn't have to share. Only his penis is referred to obliquely, metaphorically, by a name that really belongs to something else. Any pre–Hebrew school *pisher* already knows that his member is a *"shtekele,"* not a *shtekele*, and he therefore uses the term only in its irreverent, slightly contemptuous *shm*-form—*shmekele*—lest anyone think that he can't tell metaphor from reality. The parallel to the Tetragrammaton turns on his using a deformed version of a name that has been substituted for the real name that he doesn't know—and knows that he doesn't know.

Because of the difficulty of invoking the deity in such cultural circumstances, Yiddish cursing tends to shy away from blasphemy; it isn't easy to say "God damn" when saying "God" is so hard, and Yiddish—although it might occasionally *call* on God—has virtually no casually blasphemous expressions of the "Jesus Christ!" type that are so common in English. What makes *shmuck* so powerful and dirty and offensive is the fact that its role as the sine qua non of the ritual that defines the whole religion, as virtually the only aspect of creation that the language treats in the same way as it treats the Creator, allows it to stand in for all those blasphemies that are literally unspeakable in traditional Jewish life. The surface vulgarity is recognized, even if only subconsciously, as a mask for something much more serious.

III

Shmuck, THE FORM under which *shmok* has come into English, is a dialect pronunciation of the Yiddish. It has nothing to do with the German *Schmuck*, "jewelry," which is often erroneously thought of as the source of the Yiddish term. The *shmuck* that we're talking about can be found in *shmok* form as early as 1697, when it appears in the manuscript of a satirical Purim play from Altendorf, Germany. In a double entendre–filled passage that begins, "I'd really like to have a lick [instead of "a look"] at that," and ends with "*lek mikh in arsh lokh*, lick my asshole," Mordechai says, "I think that my wife's hole—I meant to say the door's hole—is too narrow" and then goes on to say that his sash or belt is "too *shmok, shmok*, I mean *shmol*"; *shmol* is Yiddish for narrow or tight-fitting. The proximity of the hole to the *shmuck* leaves no doubt as to the meaning of the word, and lets us know how well established the usage must have been: dirty jokes that need footnotes tend not to get told.

The leap from *shmok*-as-penis to *shmok*-as-fool in Yiddish is no greater than that from tool-as-penis to tool-as-fool in English. It's the idea of thinking with your dick, letting your hormones drive your hippocampus, *not* when you're looking for sex, but when you're doing your taxes or driving a car; your behavior is brainless, inappropriate, and sometimes offensive. As Max Weinreich says in his *History of the Yiddish Language*, the two-legged *shmok* is a "combination of fool, gullible person, and *nudnik*," a person of no intelligence and no discernment who behaves in a bothersome and annoying fashion.

But Weinreich, still the doyen of the academic study of Yiddish nearly forty years after his death, mentions *shmok* only in passing (while pointing out that none of the common Middle High German terms for penis ever made its way into Yiddish), and stops short of the whole ugly truth. Like real-life *shmek* that come both with and without a foreskin, the metaphorical ones can also be divided into two broad categories, only the first of which can include oneself or one's friends. It's the kind of *shmuck* that anybody who isn't always a *shmuck* has probably been at one time or another: "So there I am in my wedding gown, standing there like a *shmuck* at the top of the Empire

State Building, when his lawyer gets out of the elevator and tells me that the wedding is off."

This is the passive *shmuck*, the *shmuck* as fool or dupe: harmless but hapless, eternal victim of petty circumstance and the wiles of others, to whom shit never ceases to happen. It's the *shmuck* that is, rather than the *shmuck* that does; no matter what he might think he's doing, the truth is that it's being done to him. It's the kind of *shmuck* who buys stock from a cold call or signs up for seminar after boot camp after workshop about how to realize your inner potential; it's the smart woman who makes stupid choices, thinking that this year's bad boy or married man is going to be different from last year's. It's everyone who took out a mortgage that they knew they couldn't afford, everybody who didn't do enough figuring to find out what all that free money could end up costing. It's all of us at that critical second when hope or desire so overrides the most basic common sense, when something—money, reputation, peace of mind—seems so close to being attainable that we ignore *anything* that we have learned from experience and open ourselves up to a good plucking— physical, financial, or emotional. And always for the sake of the last thing we really need.

It isn't always our fault. Anyone with emotions is vulnerable to this kind of *shmuckery*, and there are times when it can't be avoided. When somebody has lied about honoring a contract or not committing adultery or meeting you at the top of the Empire State Building to get married, you've simply been taken advantage of by a *shmuck* who isn't playing by the rules. Being duped or deceived in this way doesn't necessarily reflect on you, unless you already know how the person in question has treated others in the past and think that this time is going to be different.

It's like Charlie Brown letting Lucy hold the football for a placekick. Even after she's given him a written guarantee promising not to do so, Lucy inevitably pulls the ball away at the last second and poor Charlie Brown ends up flat on his back. Yiddish-speaking readers give out with a mental sigh and a pitying murmur: "The poor little *shmuck*."

We're close to the origins of comedy here, maybe even the origins of humor itself. We already know what Charlie Brown can't bring himself to admit, and can laugh about it only because the emotions invested in trying to kick that ball are his, not ours: if he didn't really care about kicking the ball, none of this would be happening. Once it comes to our own lives, though, we are all the dupes of desire, and the idea that people and circumstances that are similar or even identical to those that we have experienced before are going to be different this time is a testament to the human capacity for self-delusion, a deliberate, active naïveté that is just another form of folly.

The Talmud talks about such feelings in a context that might seem a bit unusual:

> Whoever has money and lends it without witnesses violates the prohibition against placing a stumbling block before the blind [see Lev. 19:14]. Resh Lakish says: He brings a curse upon himself.
>
> (BOVO METSIYO 75B)

"The blind" here means you, the lender. In its immediate Talmudic environment it means that you're so carried away by the thought of all the interest that you're going to earn that you neglect to take the basic precautions to make sure that you get paid. In a larger sense, you're so blinded by the thought of getting what you want—generally for very little effort—that you ignore everything else and "just do it," and end up with egg all over your face.

Resh Lakish's statement about the curse refers to the inevitable lawsuit and the fact that the person to whom you've lent the money will deny ever having borrowed it. In the absence of properly witnessed documentation, you'll be able to kiss the money you loaned, along with the money that you spend on legal fees and any reputation for competence that you might have had, good-bye.

Note that self-*shmuckification* of this kind is described as a violation of divine law. We're dealing with a system in which stupidity has become a sin, and like all sins it can be avoided. All we have to do in the case just outlined is to follow the advice that we'd give anyone else by trying to run our lives on the basis of a little *seykhl*, a little rational thought, rather than pure emotion. This might not be easy, but it's nothing—a moral and emotional picnic—compared with the kind of *shmuckish* passivity that so robs its victims of any insight or willpower that they can no longer recognize their own situation, let alone do anything to improve it.

The prototype, the classic example, is found in a Yiddish short story written in 1894 by Y. L. Peretz, one of the central figures in the creation of modern Yiddish literature. Bontshe Shvayg—Silent Bontshe—the character for whom the story is named, lives a life more humble than anything that Uriah Heep (not to mention Mott the Hoople) would ever have pretended to. A porter by profession, he was mistreated as a child, abused as an adult: cheated, robbed, cuckolded, and mocked, yet Bontshe, alone of all his tribe, never once complained, never once cried out, not even, the story tells us, when the knife slipped at his circumcision.

After his death, the heavenly powers decide to reward him for his years of patient suffering. He's admitted straightaway into Paradise and told that he can have whatever he wants, anything at all; if he really wants, he can have *everything*. It's the least they can give him for a lifetime of nothing.

Bontshe can hardly believe his good luck. Although Peretz never describes what goes on in his head, readers for over a century have been seduced by their own visions of gold, silver, dancing girls, and tables laden with the most exquisite food and the rarest of wines. It's unlikely that Bontshe shares their vision; he thinks for a minute, then turns to the judge of the heavenly court and confidently reels off the whole of his wish list: a hot roll with butter for breakfast every morning.

Peretz's story was hugely controversial in its day, primarily because Bontshe was seen as a symbol of the Jewish people and Bontshe, it should be clear, is a *shmuck*. Suffering has made him stupid; he has internalized his tormentors' image of him so completely that he is literally incapable of imagining any other kind of life (or afterlife) for himself. Henoch of Alexander, a mid-nineteenth-century Polish Hasidic leader, once said, "The real exile of Israel in Egypt was that they had learned to endure it," that is, they started to think like slaves, to look at themselves in the same way as their Egyptian owners did; they lost sight of what they could be and were happy to struggle to remain the slaves that they already were.

Henoch's teacher, Menachem Mendel of Kotzk, the last and most imposing of the classical Hasidic leaders, illustrated this kind of *shmuckery* in a parable:

There was once a prince who behaved so badly that his father, the king, drove him from the palace and had him exiled to the farthest reaches of the kingdom. With no other means of earning a living, the prince hired himself out to a craftsman as an apprentice, for which he was given his food but nothing else. He went around barefoot and in tatters.

One day, the king was thinking about his son. He summoned a friend and said, "Go, find out where the prince is." Once the friend had found the prince, he asked, "What would you like me to ask your father, the king, on your behalf?"

The prince replied, "He sent me into exile. The least he could do is send me something to wear and a pair of shoes."

The king's friend said, "Idiot! You were supposed to say, 'Ask my father to take me back.' Then you would have had everything."

The prince and Charlie Brown, Bontshe and someone who lends money without witnesses, are the type of minor-league *shmuck* known in Yiddish by the name of *shmendrik*. In a language known for its versatility in insult, *shmendrik* is among the most versatile of insults. The *shmendrik* embodies the kind of metaphysical cluelessness about one's own nature and that of the surrounding world that leads the British to describe the same sort of person as "a tit in a trance." Yiddish rarely mentions the titmouse, which often hangs upside down in order to

feed, but the idea of going about something in the completely
wrong manner without any apparent consciousness of the fact
that the rest of the world—those who succeed at whatever activity the *shmendrik* is failing at—does things differently, lends
an aptness to the comparison.

A *shmendrik* is anybody from Bob Dylan's Mr. Jones in
"Ballad of a Thin Man," who knows that something is happening here, but "don't know what it is," to Rupert Pupkin,
the hapless asshole played by Robert De Niro in *The King of
Comedy*. At the end of the movie, Pupkin, a thirty-one-year-
old messenger and completely talentless aspiring comic who
lives with his mother, explains why he has kidnapped talk-
show host Jerry Langford and demanded a spot on Langford's
show as ransom for Langford's safe return. In the movie's
best-known line, Pupkin gives such perfect voice to the painful mixture of impotence and delusion that characterizes the
shmendrik that you almost feel sorry for him: "Better to be
king for a night," he says, "than *shmuck* for a lifetime." If only
it were really possible.

The *shmendrik* has a bumbling quality, an incompetence
that is almost endearing, as long as it isn't directed at you. He
or she differs from the *nebbish*, a seeming milquetoast of a
person for whom you feel immediately sorry, not only in that
being a *nebbish* is more a matter of appearance than actual attainment or ability (think of *nebbish* as the specifically Jewish
forerunner of the more pluralistic nerd), but also, and more
importantly, because the *shmendrik*, like the paranoiac, bases
his or her life on a delusion, generally one of ability. Where the
nebbish might do something very well, but wear a misbuttoned
shirt while doing it, the *shmendrik* can be immaculately tai-

lored, but never stops walking into walls. It is significant that *shmendrik* is also used by women to refer to a penis (I mean the real thing) for which they feel no warmth and by which they are not impressed. "A whole night of Viagra and he still couldn't get the *shmendrik* to stand up long enough to do it," or, "Go ahead. If that's all you want, put the *shmendrik* in and get it over with."

A *shmendrik* is a certain breed of *shmuck*, limply ineffectual and unconscious of this limitation. Like Charlie Brown, the *shmendrik* considers himself on top of things, and just *knows* that this time, things are going to be different. He suffers from delusions of understanding, illusions that things are now under control. The Federal Emergency Management Agency's response to Hurricane Katrina and the Buffalo snowstorm of 2006, along with its faked California press conference in 2007, are textbook examples of what it means to be a *shmendrik*.

The *shmendrik* is as harmless a *shmuck* as you're ever going to find, and we can class all sorts of day-to-day *nudniks*—tedious pests—under its rubric. If you're not dressed as a pirate or B-movie hooker right now, while reading this sentence; if you mention your tedious personal hobbyhorse—whether it's the Kennedy assassination, brewed condiments, or Engelbert Humperdinck's superiority to Tom Jones—only on your blog and not in live conversation; if you've refused to allow someone who has cheated you once an opportunity to do so again, then you probably aren't a *shmendrik*. Or not much of one, at least.

Before we go on to describe the more active kinds of *shmuck*, though, it is probably a good idea to take a more detailed look at what a *shmuck* is not.

TWO

What's a *Mentsh*?

I

LIKE *shmuck, mentsh* is a Yiddish word. Fundamentally, it means "person, human being," and applies to everyone on earth. So, for instance, you could say that John *iz a mentsh on a gal*, a good-natured guy, or Mary *iz a mentsh on a gal*, a good-natured gal. Every human being is some sort of *mentsh*: John is a *mentsh*, Mary is a *mentsh*, even little Tommy, busy pulling the tail of their dog, Farfel, is a *mentsh*. Farfel is an innocent victim who deserves our pity, but he is an animal, not a *mentsh*.

In this sense, we are all *mentshn*. Regardless of our capacities, attitudes, or deportment, we are all human beings, just as Warner Bros.' Porky, E. B. White's Wilbur, and Arnold Ziffle are pigs. It's strictly a matter of biology. But the Yiddish way of thinking has never been content to leave biology alone—just look what psychoanalysis managed to do to humping—and it long ago extended the meaning of *mentsh* well beyond "feather-less, rational biped" to "featherless, rational biped who knows how to behave like a featherless, rational biped." As they say in Yiddish, "*A mentsh iz a mentsh vayl er iz a mentsh*"—a *mentsh* is a *mentsh* because he's a *mentsh*.

Extending *mentsh*'s field of meaning from biological classi-fication to moral attainment is a uniquely Yiddish development, without any parallel in the German from which the word *mentsh* derives. Only in Yiddish does *mentsh* mean "decent, respectable, upstanding person; honest, honorable person; man or woman of integrity; person of moral substance." If my mother had said, "*Sei ein mensch*, be a *mensch*," to me in German (an event about as likely as her coming home with a honey-glazed ham in her brand-new Volkswagen), it would have meant, "Michael, my son, stop being a tortoise."

Since we're going to be speaking about a meaning that doesn't exist in German, I've decided to avoid the more familiar, but to-tally German spelling, *mensch*, which carries none of the mean-ings that we're going to look at in this book, and instead spell *mentsh* according to the standard Yiddish transliteration system developed by the YIVO Institute of Jewish Research.

If there is some record that indicates even approximately when Yiddish first took *mentsh* beyond its narrowly taxo-nomic German usage, it isn't immediately accessible. Alex-ander Harkavy's 1910 Yiddish-English dictionary defines *mentsh* as only "1) man; 2) employee, servant," although his 1928 *Yiddish-English-Hebrew Dictionary* expands this to "human being, man; person; servant, employee." Uriel Wein-reich's *Modern English-Yiddish/Yiddish-English Dictionary*, first published in 1968, adds one more meaning to Harkavy's second list: "responsible/mature person." To say, though, that the meaning of "responsible/mature person" must therefore have developed sometime between 1928 and 1968 would be as absurd as to claim that *mentsh* began to mean "human being" only between 1910 and 1928.

Harkavy and Weinreich were both first-rate scholars to whom everybody working in Yiddish owes an incalculable debt, but there is only so much that anybody can cram into a one-volume dictionary. There *is* a multivolume, comprehensive dictionary of Yiddish, but it is "comprehensive" only in the way that a "big fucking deal" is large and sexually active: *Der Groyser Verterbukh fun der Yidisher Shprakh* (*The Great Dictionary of the Yiddish Language*) has actually managed to improve on Dorothy Parker's description of Katharine Hepburn's acting style as running "the gamut of emotions from A to B."

As most readers probably know already, Yiddish is written in the Hebrew alphabet, which has twenty-two letters, beginning with *aleph*. *Mentsh* starts with *mem*, the thirteenth letter, and is not found in *The Great Dictionary*, which begins with *aleph* and ends with *aleph*. *The Great Dictionary* covers the alphabet from A to A. Material for the remaining letters was assembled a long time ago and has been lying in a sort of lexicographical limbo ever since, neither published nor discarded, as inaccessible to the public as if the editors' mothers had tossed it all out with the editors' old comic books.

There are competing stories about how this came to pass. The version that seems to keep lawyers from the door is that it was strictly a matter of money. It ran out in 1961 or 1980-something, and despite the growing academic interest in Yiddish, the chairs that have sprung up at various universities, and Aaron

Lansky's remarkable success in establishing and raising funds for the National Yiddish Book Center in Amherst, Massachusetts, the dictionary has been unable to find enough donors to fund a monument of scholarship that would make everybody's work in the field easier, deeper, and more accurate.

The one that rings true poetically, whether it really happened or not, also helps to remind us of the undeniable fact that Yiddish-speaking Jews can violate the principles outlined in this book as well as anybody else: a bitter argument over the use of the silent *aleph* in spelling certain words led to a period of prolonged inactivity, which led in turn to a loss of funding.

Whatever really happened, the materials are not in the public domain and access to them is severely restricted. So the only glimmer of hope for dealing with twenty-one twenty-seconds of the Yiddish alphabet resides in the fact that Yiddish makes frequent use of prefixes, so many of which begin with *aleph* that it has been estimated that the four volumes devoted to that letter contain about a third of all the material that was supposed to have been published. So even though the *Verterbukh* never gets as far as *mentsh*, it contains such verbs as *oysmentshlen*, *avekmentshlen*, *oysmentshen*, and *oyfmentshlen*, all of which describe different stages in the process of turning a raw hunk of humanity into a *mentsh*, and can therefore give us a fairly clear idea of the basic outlines of *mentsh*-hood.

The type of person who emerges could be described as kosher. Kosher here does not mean that she is necessarily Jewish or devoted to Jewish ritual law, forget about readily edible by Jews; the basic meaning of kosher is "proper, fit for, appropriate, worthy." A kosher person, then, is someone whose conduct is fitting, proper, appropriate; someone who knows how to behave in human society and can get herself through life without treading on other people's feet. Just remember that kosher in Latin would be *decens*—from which we get the English *decent*. A kosher person is a decent person, a person of integrity who can hold her head up in society because she has nothing to be ashamed of.

Being a *mentsh* involves more than refraining from shameful behavior, though; you don't get any awards for not committing murder or neglecting to rob a bank, and plenty of otherwise decent people accepted segregation or South African apartheid as the natural course of life, without ever trying to do anything about them. Merely holding yourself back from doing the wrong things is not enough. A *mentsh* has to do the right things, and must understand the difference between right and wrong in order to do so: right and wrong in an absolute sense and right and wrong in a given situation, especially one in which all possible actions might be equally moral but some could still be very wrong.

A *mentsh* also needs to be self-sufficient, able to provide for himself in normal circumstances without having to rely on the kindness of others. He stands on his own two feet, knows the limits of individual effort, and—if circumstances should demand it—ain't too proud to beg:

> Having been told of a man who died of starvation, a certain *tzaddik* [Hasidic leader] responded, "No, he died of pride because he was unwilling to ask others for food."

"Who is wise?" asks the Talmud. "He who foresees the outcome of his actions" (*Tomid* 32a). A *mentsh* understands the necessity of doing the right thing at the right time.

A *mentsh*, then, is a person who knows how to live with others as well as with herself, a person fit for human society. A friend will tell a friend just as easily as a parent tells a child, "*Zay a mentsh*, be a *mentsh*"; that is, do what you know you're supposed to do. Don't sit paralyzed by indecision; don't feel sorry for yourself because that two-hour visit to your aunt in the hospital is going to overlap with the season finale of your favorite TV show and you're so deprived that you don't even have TiVo; go visit that neighbor you don't like whose husband just died. To be a *mentsh* is to do what you know to be your human duty, even when the obligation is at odds with your own preferences.

II

To KNOW WHAT your duty is, though, you already have to be a *mentsh*; and the first thing that you'll notice about any *mentsh* is that he is not a kid. There's a well-known Yiddish proverb that holds that a parent's duty is to make *mentshn* out of children—to turn undeveloped raw material into men and women who can turn around and do the same thing in their turn.

A child might do the right thing, but it isn't considered capable of doing so for the right reasons until it has reached a certain age:

> "A poor but wise boy is better than an old and foolish king" (Ecclesiastes 4:13). "A poor but wise boy"—this is the inclination to do good.
>
> Why is it called a boy?
>
> It only joins itself to a person at the age of thirteen.

Why is he called poor?

Not everyone listens to him.

And why is he called wise?

Because he teaches human beings the proper path.

"An old and foolish king"—this is the evil urge.

Why is he called a king?

Everybody listens to him.

Why is he called old?

He stays with a person from birth to death.

Why is he called foolish?

He teaches human beings the paths of evil.

And why is he described as not knowing how to take counsel? Because he does not know how much sorrow and suffering he brings upon himself and therefore takes no precautions against them.

(ECCLESIASTES RABBO 4:9)

No wonder Yiddish-speaking parents never compliment their children; the little devil on the kid's left shoulder has yet to be balanced by a preachy little angel on the right: a kid who isn't following direct adult orders can only do the right thing by virtue of prior adult instruction or by accident. Jewish tradition looks at childhood as something to be got through, like boot camp or a lengthy dental appointment. Youth is a liability—just ask any kid—a forced layover on the path to adulthood and responsibility. While twelve-hour school days and slapstick notions of discipline certainly contributed to this desire to graduate into maturity, the same impulse can be seen today—better, can be heard—in any

Hasidic community, where little boys do their best to mimic the singing and gestures, not of their fathers, but of their grandfathers and the other old guys at *shul*.

The traditional Jewish view of childhood is that we're born stupid and have to be nudged along into *mentsh*-hood. Twenty-four hours after a boy turns thirteen (twelve years and a day for girls), childhood comes to a sudden end. Not that anyone has ever considered a thirteen-year-old kid anything other than a *pisher* who'd best keep to his place, but now that he is old enough to count for a minyan, the traditional quorum of ten men needed for communal prayer, he is as much a full-fledged citizen as any unmarried person can be, and he damned well better act like one: "If a boy is Bar Mitzvah and still likes to play, people make fun of him and tell him that he is supposed to be a *mentsh*. And girls the same thing." Traditional Jewish society would react with undisguised horror to our notion of an inner child: "What, we're born with *two* assholes now?"

Still, childhood plays a crucial role in the growth of the idea of a *mentsh*. The Yiddish *mentsh* seems to have evolved from its German forebear on the far side of the door to the *kheyder*, the traditional Jewish elementary school. The basic study technique in such schools still consists of reading a passage from the Bible and translating it from the original Hebrew into Yiddish: if we make allowance for the fact that the Bible is not really in English, the beginning of Genesis would come out as, "In the beginning, *in onheyb*, God created, *az got hot bashafn*, the heavens and the earth, *di himlen un di erd*." Any necessary explanations are also added; if these come verbatim from traditional sources, those other sources are quoted and translated in their turn.

Students soon learn that the Yiddish *mentsh* can represent at least four different biblical words that mean "man" or
"person." According to the proverb, "*Odem* is a *mentsh* and *ish*
is a *mentsh* and *enoysh* is a *mentsh* and *geyver* is a *mentsh*";
but, we're warned, "a *mentsh* isn't always a *mentsh*"—a human
being isn't always a *mentsh*. The first two Hebrew words,
odem (which gives us "Adam") and *ish* (think of the *Is* in Judas
Iscariot) are the ones that really concern us. The third, *enoysh*
(whence the English name Enos), is pretty much synonymous
with *odem* (most commentators say that it places more emphasis on the lowliness of the human condition), while *geyver* is
limited to males and can also mean "cock" or "rooster."

Odem refers to the entire human species, regardless of age or
sex. So we find "from the first-born human [*odem*] to the first-
born animal" (Exod. 13:15); and "whoever kills a human being
[*odem*] will surely be put to death" (Lev. 24:17). An *ish* is an adult
male; its female counterpart is *isho*. Although some meanings of
ish depend on the presence of a penis ("husband," for instance),
others can easily be extended to either sex, since Hebrew uses
the masculine form to refer to any indefinite person: "someone,"
"anybody," "nobody," "somebody." The "whoever" in the verse
from Leviticus just quoted provides a fine example of this use of
ish. No one has ever claimed that the use of *ish* as the subject here
means that murder is forbidden only to males.

There is an equally unambiguous example of this indefinite
usage at the beginning of the second chapter of I Kings, when the
dying King David charges his son, Solomon, and says:

I am going the way of all the earth; be strong and be an *ish*.
And keep the charge of the Lord your God to walk in His

ways and keep His statutes, commandments, ordinances,
and testimonies as they are written in the Torah of Moses,
so that you may prosper in whatever you might do and
wherever you might turn.

(I KINGS 2:2–3)

I have yet to see an English translation that doesn't render
ish here as "man," yet nothing that Solomon has to do in order
to be an *ish* is anything that a woman could not have done
just as well, even in biblical times. Therefore David Kimhi, a
prominent medieval exegete and grammarian, explains that
ish in this verse means "being diligent, controlling yourself
and subduing your baser impulses," an interpretation echoed
roughly seven hundred years later by Rabbi Meir Weisser.
Weisser, better known as the Malbim, was chief rabbi of Bu-
charest for a short time, turned down a chance to be chief rabbi
of New York, and spent a good deal of time explaining the differences in meaning and nuance between apparently synonymous Hebrew words. According to him, *ish* is often used "to
designate generality, not gender"—everybody, not just certain
somebodies—and can refer to someone who "exercises control."

Odem and *ish* crop up frequently in the Bible and Talmud,
often in exactly the kind of moralizing passages that we've just
seen: the *mentshly* ideal is not something that was confined to
any particular segment or group in Yiddish-speaking Jewish
society. The idea was the common property of all Yiddish-
speakers, regardless of their religious or political attitudes. It
originated in the basic curriculum that was common to the
entire Yiddish-speaking world, then took on a life of its own

outside of the classroom among grown-ups who had studied there as kids. These people were rich and poor, bright and dull, old and young, male and female, conservative and liberal. They might have suffered at the hands of people—Jewish and other-wise—who were not *mentshn*, but they never lost their respect for *mentshn* with whom they might disagree about everything except the necessity of being a *mentsh*.

Although the idea of *mentsh*-hood is rooted in religious edu-cation, religious practice itself is far from crucial in determining whether or not a person is a *mentsh*. At one time, traditional ob-servance was taken for granted if you were speaking about a Jew and, of course, dismissed out of hand if you were not. Otherwise, neither faith nor unbelief tends to matter very much, so long as the person in question is a *mentsh* in other respects. A venerable Yiddish proverb states, "Better a Jew without a beard than a beard without a Jew." Equally venerable and even more pointed is, "A goat has a beard, too, and it's still just a goat": that is, better a *mentsh* who isn't religious than a religious person who isn't a *mentsh*. Since the days of the Prophets, we've been told that if you don't observe the commandments that govern relations between people, God isn't going to be too impressed by the care that you take in fulfilling more ceremonial obligations.

An image of the day-to-day *mentsh*, who might or might not be rich, religious, or intelligent, is found in the book of Kings, where we are told that during the reign of Solomon, "Judah and Israel dwelt in safety, *ish* under his own vine and under his own fig tree" (1 Kings 5:5, in the Hebrew), that is, each person under their vine or fig tree: their own, not their neighbor's; their own, with no eye to acquiring someone else's and no thought of enlarging their vineyard or orchard at the expense of anyone else. Substitute "job" for "vine" and "bank account" for "fig tree" and you'll see that it isn't as easy to sit contentedly as the Bible makes it sound; a *mentsh*, in short, is someone who does his best to treat other people as well as he treats himself.

III

THERE IS AN old joke that sums up the traditional Jewish attitude to almost everything. In the version that was going around when I was a kid, a little boy runs up to his *zeyde*, his grandfather, and says excitedly, "*Zeyde, zeyde!* Did you hear? Sandy Koufax just shut out the Twins and won the World Series!"

The grandfather looks at the boy with world-weary rue and says, "So? It's good for the Jews?"

This is internal satire, of course, Jew-on-Jew mockery of the Jewish preoccupation with survival and the occasional tendency to judge everything against narrow communal standards of "good for the Jews" or "bad for the Jews." It's a typical— and justified—concern on the part of members of any unpopular minority group, made into a cultural touchstone by people who were *always* an unpopular minority. I can still remember the first words that I heard from a grown-up when the news reached us that President Kennedy had been assassinated: "Please God, don't let it be a Jew [who shot him]." I heard the same thing when George Wallace was shot. The fear in both cases was something entirely separate from the attitude of individual Jews to the people who'd been shot; there was a pervasive dread that the entire Jewish community would be held responsible, should the shooter turn out to be Jewish.

The history of the Jews in the West has been defined by the Christian notion of collective guilt, and Jews remain sensitive to the idea that all of us will be blamed for the actions of any of us, or that one of us in a position of power will be accused of acting in the interests of the Jews instead of the nation. One of the more convoluted expressions of this attitude that I've encountered was the relief expressed after 9/11 by many Democrats whom I know that Joe Lieberman had not become vice president, after all; they were afraid that the presence of a Jew in so high an office—any Jew—would only have complicated an already horrible situation.

When "bad for the Jews" so often equaled carnage or expulsion, "good for the Jews"—which almost nothing ever was— became an ironic rhetorical question that meant, "That's all very nice, but I really don't care." For years now I've yearned to be a judge on some reality television show, one of those in which people sing, dance, or do whatever else they do in order to become celebrities, just to make "So, it's good for the Jews?" into a nationally popular catchphrase.

Again, as an expression that satirizes the Jewish preoccupation with other Jews and with how we're all perceived by the people around us, "good for the Jews" is a less serious version of the one unvarying and inflexible rule that characterized Ashkenazic Jewish society until very, very recently: it is incumbent on every member of the community to behave in such a way as to help maintain the community from within while doing nothing intentionally to increase the enmity from without—always to act in a way that is good for the Jews. While the latter part of this rule was sometimes taken as a warning against Jewing it up too much in public—*nisht far di goyim*, "not in front of the gentiles," has been a byword for a very long time and has certainly been used by less tolerant members of the Jewish community to promote a particularly small-minded, petit bourgeois, Grundy-ish version of our culture—the former part helps to explain the development of *mentsh*-hood as a community ideal.

The schools in which *mentsh* was used to translate the Hebrew words mentioned above were part of a society that operated as a countercultural parallel to the larger Christian society around it. They were there to educate their students for adversity, to impart not only the facts and ritual knowl-edge necessary for the proper practice of Judaism, but also a notion of the kind of life to which acting on this knowledge was supposed to lead. A society in a near-constant state of macro-emergency had to be sure that it was at least able to cope with the micro-emergencies that constitute so large a part of any individual life.

One of the most important ways in which it did so was to emphasize history in a way that ignored the passage of time and made every contemporary Jew a participant in the mythic events that brought the nation into being. Every participant at every Passover seder for a good couple of millennia now has read a quotation from the Mishna and the rabbinic commen-tary that accompanies it:

> In every generation, a *mentsh* [*odem* in Hebrew] is obliged to see himself as if he, too, had come out of Egypt. As it is said: "And you shall tell your son on that day, 'This [the seven days of eating matzoh] is because of what the Lord did for *me* when *I* left Egypt' [Exod. 13:8]."
>
> (PESOKHIM 10:5)

The Holy One, Blessed Be He, not only delivered our ancestors from Egypt, but He also delivered us with them, as it says: "In order to bring *us*, to give *us* the land that He had promised to our ancestors" [Deut. 6:23] [my emphasis].

As if our current suffering weren't enough, we're supposed to internalize the torments of our forebears and suffer them, too. And why? Because one day, we believe, the suffering will stop and everything will be hunky-dory, and as long as we continue to think of ourselves as escaped slaves who are really here only by the grace of God, we'll be damned sure never to treat others the way that others might have treated us. We shouldn't take such prosperity as we have for granted, nor should we complain too much about our current plight, whatever it might be—we who have gone out of Egypt have lived through plenty worse and should never forget it. We should also remember that it was mercy that got us out of there, not any particular merits of our own.

So strong is this latter feeling that the Bible commands the Jewish people to respect their enemies and erstwhile oppressors, which could explain why so many Jewish Community Center parking lots are full of BMWs and Audis: "You shall not abhor an Edomite, for he is your brother; you shall not abhor an Egyptian, for you were an alien in his land" (Deut. 23:8). Badly as they might have acted, their bad behavior is not allowed to negate their good deeds in any way. As Rashi, whose eleventh-century commentary is still the inevitable accompaniment to any *kheyder*-level reading of the Bible, says, *"Do not abhor an Edomite*—completely, even though you might be justified in abhorring him because he came to greet you with a sword [see Numbers, chapter 20]. *Do not abhor an Egyptian*—entirely, even though they threw your male children into the river. And why not abhor them? They gave you lodging in your time of need."

We are commanded to take the merits of our enemies into consideration and to give credit even to those whose virtues we would prefer to ignore. You don't have to like them, but you have to admit that you owe them. The principle is given more general application in the Talmud, which quotes the proverb, "Do not throw a rock into a well from which you have drunk," in connection with this biblical verse (*Bovo Kamo* 92b).

This sort of consideration for others, the constant reminder that they and their needs are just as real as you and yours, lies at the very root of the way in which Jewish people are supposed to deal with the peculiar burdens placed upon them by their covenant with the Lord. Too many people are looking for the easy way out, for a way to fulfill the commandments with the least possible amount of effort. But that isn't the way that it's supposed to be:

Rabbi Elazar ben Azariah said, Where does Scripture let us know that a *mentsh* [*odem*] is not supposed to say, "I have no desire to wear linen mixed with wool; I have no desire to eat pork; I have no desire to have forbidden sexual relations," but should say instead, "I want to do all these things, but what can I do when my Father in Heaven has ruled otherwise?" We know so because it is implied in the verse, "I have separated you from the peoples, so that you might be mine" (Lev. 20:26); that is, one separates oneself from transgression and accepts the yoke of heaven.

(SIFRA, KEDOSHIM 9:12)

It's exactly what's going on with the Egyptians in the biblical quotation: you want to hate them, but heaven or your conscience tells you that you have to do otherwise. The only way that you're going to know what that heavenly voice is trying to tell you is to go to school and learn what the Torah tells us.

IV

THE REST OF this book is designed to provide the relevant parts of that education both for Jewish people who might not have received old-style, ethically centered instruction in Judaism and for people who aren't Jewish at all but are interested in learning new techniques for making everybody's lives a little bit better. We need to have a look at a couple of more aspects of traditional Jewish society, though, in order to be able to understand that education in context and see how and why it developed into something of universal utility and application.

As everybody knows, the Jews have no pope. There is no synod or council, no official hierarchy of rabbis that can make rulings that are binding on all Jews everywhere. There has been no Sanhedrin, no Jewish Supreme Court, for seventeen hundred years, and the Elders of Zion are merely an anti-Semitic wet dream. The truth is that if enough people oppose all rabbis on a given issue, the people are going to win every time. Such beloved Jewish customs as saying Kaddish in memory of a departed relative or waving a chicken around your head three times on the eve of Yom Kippur met with considerable rabbinic opposition at different times and places, yet are accepted today in even the most orthodox circles, which are where most of the chicken-swinging takes place. Judaism is based on consensus rather than decree, and as such has historically tended to follow the middle path between extremes of opinion.

Take the mezuzah, for example, the case holding a small scroll of biblical passages that is affixed to so many Jewish doorposts. In discussing whether it is to be hung horizontally or vertically, Moses Isserles, author of those parts of the *Shulkhan Arukh*, the authoritative code of Jewish law, that set the rules for Ashkenazic (rather than Sephardic) Jews, says explicitly:

> The truly punctilious follow both opinions by placing it [the mezuzah] on a diagonal slant.
>
> (SHULKHAN ARUKH, YOREH DEAH 289:4)

The earlier authorities who argued for a strictly horizontal or strictly vertical orientation are outside in the cold together, while we punctilious Ashkenazim warm ourselves by the fire of a compromise that satisfies none of the original disputants but has been sanctified by the simple passage of time.

Think of life as a birthday party for your younger brother or sister. As a four-year-old, you're young enough to get some kind of consolation present, if only to keep you from getting too jealous, but you still don't get the party that you'd like to have for yourself. Your kid brother or sister gets a party and presents, but they're still upset that you, whose birthday it most emphatically is not, get anything at all, and they are insisting that any presents go to them, the birthday kid. Your parents point out that neither of you has any reason to whine: you both have more than you did before the party, and only a baby expects 100 percent.

Normative Judaism has no place for babies. Until such time

as they became able to deliver the balance of power in Israeli elections, zealots and ideologues were stringently ignored; the community as a whole was familiar enough with Jewish history to know that zealots and ideologues were responsible for the loss of our country and our apparently endless exile. Post-Temple Judaism is therefore uniquely accommodating, so much so that it has turned the passive-aggressive compromise into a veritable art form. It isn't that everybody gets what they want, it's that *nobody* gets what they want, but everyone doesn't get it in roughly equal measure.

The Talmud speaks quite openly about the difference between such biblical regulations as the prohibition against pork, which are never going to change, and those of a more purely social nature that could tear a society apart if applied, and finds plenty of room for fine-tuning the latter. So, in a well-known passage that is frequently quoted by anti-Semites bent on proving that the Talmud is the source of all evil, we are told that "Rabbi Joshua ben Levi said, 'Money makes bastards kosher'" (*Kiddushin* 71a). "Bastards" (*mamzeyrim* in the original) has nothing to do with birth outside of wedlock; it is a legal term used to describe children born of incestuous or adulterous unions who are, strictly speaking, allowed to marry only converts or other bastards. Rabbi Joshua is talking about wealthy *mamzeyrim* whose money has allowed them to marry into "pure" families, despite the hereditary defect that they are supposed to be carrying. Rashi, who is the foremost commentator on the Talmud as well as the Bible, says, "They have been absorbed into the larger community on account of their wealth, which has allowed them to be 'purified' in the sense that in future the Lord will no longer separate them from the

mainstream community because too many mainstream families will have attached themselves to them."

In other words, reality wins every time. When the consensus
of reasonable people opposes a prescribed mode of behavior,
the prescription is adjusted accordingly. Indeed, it is forbidden
to pass any law or decree that is certain not to be observed
(*Bovo Kamo* 79b); instituting such a law will only bring about
disrespect for the lawmakers, whose more reasonable rulings
will end up being ignored as well, and turn fundamentally law-
abiding people into sinners. Even the most teetotaling of rabbis
would have advised against Prohibition.

V

IN SUCH A system, where the fait accompli is ultimately more
powerful than any argument, care has to be taken about which
faits become *accomplis* and the way in which they become so.
Traditional Jewish society operated on the basis of a number of
shared assumptions and beliefs, and what we now think of as
religious behavior was as much a sign of ethnicity—of where
you belonged—as anything else; men got up in the morning,
put on prayer shawls and phylacteries, and recited the morning
prayers, not because they were religious but because they were
Jews and that's what Jewish men do in the morning. Think of
Jewish life as a game of sandlot baseball with the *Shulkhan
Arukh* as the rule book. There's no real umpire, no ref of any
kind, because everybody is assumed to know how to play.
Local traditions, lot-specific variants of the standard rules, are
explained as the progress of the game demands, and woe to any
neighborhood kid who tries to sneak by to go to the library or

the movies; once the game gets going, they have no choice but to play.

Being Jewish in the traditional society of Yiddish-speaking Eastern Europe was a twenty-four-hour-a-day affair, something that determined every aspect of your life. The various codes of Jewish law, culminating in the *Shulkhan Arukh,* ran your life, and their rules extend far beyond the realm of ritual. The first four chapters of the *Shulkhan Arukh* are called: The Law of Getting Up in the Morning; The Law of Getting Dressed; Behavior in the Washroom; Laws of Hand-washing. The *Shulkhan Arukh* tells you how to get out of bed; how to put on your clothes; how to go to the toilet; how, when, and where to have sex; who not to have it with; and many other things that outsiders might consider either inconsequential or matters of strictly individual preference.

Most of the Jews who performed these activities in strict accordance with the book's demands had probably never seen a copy and would not have been able to understand it if they had. These practices were passed along as the natural way of doing things, something you learned as a kid and continued to do for the rest of your life, teaching them to your own children in turn, and so on down the generations. The most you were likely to know was that if the *Shulkhan Arukh* doesn't tell you how to do what you're doing, you probably shouldn't be doing it.

The motive underlying this apparent mania for codifying even the minutest details of human behavior, the real purpose of all this regimentation, is a desire—an obsession, really—to make every conceivable activity that isn't sinful or criminal into something more than itself, to invest it with meaning and purpose beyond its own performance and confer dignity even on something as lowly as taking a crap. The blessing that accompanies this activity explains how people have been created with "holes upon holes and orifices upon orifices," and that "if one of these were to rupture or another to be stopped, it would be impossible to remain alive and stand before [God] for even a single hour," that is, we couldn't continue to be ourselves if the Lord were to deregulate our physical functions. Everybody knows this, but a Jew was never allowed to forget it. Jews have always known that other people don't approach all of these activities in a similar spirit, but such lack of knowledge in no way detracts from the essentially meaningful nature of the activity itself.

Pausing to make a bit of a fuss over everything—what Yiddish calls a *tsimmes*—also helps to remind us that there are more important things than our own immediate needs or petty desires. The discipline of having to make a short blessing before you eat and a very long one afterward, no matter how hungry you are or how much of a rush you're in to get back to work, reminds you that you are not the center of the universe and that the universe, in turn, does not exist solely to satisfy your desires.

Classical Jewish culture is all about weighing and measuring, putting things in their proper places in proper proportions. As a religion based on mitzvahs—commandments that prohibit some activities and make others obligatory—Judaism is above all a religion of action, of performance and activity. While the outside world might look at being Jewish as a state of being— something that you *are*—the internal attitude of the culture is somewhat different.

From the Jewish point of view—the one that matters—being Jewish is a matter of how you think and what you do. Being born to a Jewish mother or converting anytime thereafter is simply the admission ticket to a lifelong party in which the dancing never stops. Judaism is something that you do all the time, and it draws virtually every human activity into the same vortex of permission and prohibition. So the daily prayer service opens with a couple of statements adapted from the Talmud that tell us what we're allowed to do ad libitum, as much as we want to, and also lets us know which commandments will help us heap up treasure in heaven even though they might not always seem to be doing us much good on earth:

These are things to which no limit has been set: the size of the corner parts of fields that are left open for the poor; that of the offering of first-fruits to be brought to the Temple; the number of times one can go to the Temple during the year; the amount of charity and other good deeds for which neither repayment nor recompense is sought; and the study of the Torah.

These are things whose fruits are eaten in this world, even while their dividends are paid in the next. And they are as follows: honoring your father and mother; giving charity and performing similar beneficent acts; getting to the synagogue early both morning and evening; hospitality; visiting the sick; providing for [poor] brides; escorting the dead to burial; devotion in prayer; bringing peace between a person and his fellow and between man and wife—and the study of Torah is equal to them all.

(PEAH 1:1; SHABBOS 127A)

Aside from the study of Torah and getting to the synagogue on time, the only strictly ritual activities mentioned depend on the existence of the Temple and have not been performed by anybody for the last couple of thousand years. All the others are the kinds of apparently colorless good deeds that would appear not to need any support or authorization from a canonical text. You don't need to have heard of the Ten Commandments to treat your parents well, nor do you need to own a pair of phylacteries to make a charitable donation. So what are these doing here? Why doesn't the text mention things like eating kosher food, keeping the Sabbath, circumcising male babies, and all the other things for which Jews are so well known?

The answer, strange as it sounds, is because these instructions aren't really intended for individuals—or, at least, not for isolated individuals. Although Judaism is all about what you do, it's also about who you do it with. It is a stubbornly communal religion that revolves in large part around the idea of having nine other Jews around to form a community. Traditionally, these were all males, and any settlement that did not have at least ten male Jews aged at least thirteen years and one day was considered a random collection of Jewish families living in close proximity to each other, but did not qualify as a congregation.

One of the main differences between a community and a group of individuals was that once the community made itself known to the secular authorities (to whom the Jews often had to appeal for the right to settle in the first place), it was permitted a fair degree of autonomy and was allowed to set up whatever institutions and organizations it needed to keep itself going. As historian I. A. Agus puts it:

The professional rabbi was entirely unknown in the Rhine communities of the early Middle Ages. . . . Religious as well as secular authority was vested in the "community" which acted as legislator, judge and administrator. When a serious religious problem arose, some residents of the town were inclined to decide one way, while others disagreed, thereby displaying the lack of a centralized religious authority. . . . [These Jews] were therefore left to their own devices, and were forced to organize every phase of their social, economic, and political life on the basis of their own law.

Even later, when each town would have at least one professional rabbi, we must never forget that these rabbis were community employees who could be fired if the community found them unsatisfactory in any way. In every case, the community decided what kind of institutions to maintain and how much money—or what percentage of the money that they had—to devote to them. A list of typical institutions reads like an embodiment of the list of mitzvahs in the prayer that we just quoted. In a community of any size, you'd find most, if not all of the following:

bikker khoylim—visiting and providing necessities for the sick

hakhnoses kale—wedding clothes and provisions for indigent brides

khevre kadishe—funeral and burial society

hakhnoses orkhim—hostel for travelers with no money for an inn (generally a bench in the study house)

moës khitin—Passover food for those who can't afford it
gmiles khasodim—free loan society
talmud toyre—free Hebrew school for children whose
    parents cannot afford tuition
malbish arumim—free clothing for the indigent
beys yesoymim—orphanage
hekdesh—poorhouse
moyshev zkeynim—home for the aged

Of the eleven different funds and institutions listed here, the first seven are referred to directly in the text of the prayer, while the last four all fall under the more general rubric of *gmiles khasodim* (defined here as the free loan society), interpreted more literally as "good deeds for which no repayment or recompense is sought." Helping those in need wasn't just a nice thing to do, it was what God wanted the entire community to do. Failure would bring trouble—big trouble, little trouble, some kind of trouble—with the Imageless Being Upstairs, and the fact that everybody had to recite the prayer every morning of their lives helped to make sure that no one was going to forget it: while you might prefer not to have to depend upon such undesired largesse, at least you know that the only way you're going to starve is if there is no food for anybody else, either.

And finally we get to the point: traditional Jewish society was based completely on the idea of mutual cooperation, of everybody looking out for everybody else. Think of London during the Blitz or New York City immediately after 9/11, then imagine that tragic solidarity and disaster-born benevolence continuing for centuries. *That* was Jewish life in much of Europe before 1939, when the assailed were finally exterminated.

If nothing else, life in a constant state of siege—even when the siege is cultural rather than physical—helps to encourage strong feelings of in-group solidarity. The idea of sharing a common destiny that could end up being determined by a common enemy can bring people together, even if only to prevent that enemy from becoming the author of their fate: there are no atheists in foxholes and no non-Jewish Jews in a pogrom. The idea that we can't escape from one another is elaborated in two separate Talmudic comments on the biblical verse, "Each one will stumble over his brother" (i.e., each other, Lev. 26:37, translated literally). The first says, "Each [will stumble] over the sin of his brother, which teaches that they are all responsible one for the other" (*Sanhedrin* 27b), while the second goes on to explain, "All of Israel are responsible [or: are guarantors] for each other" (*Shvuos* 39a).

This idea of responsibility is generally interpreted in two ways. The most obvious is that Jewish people watch out for each other; that tribal loyalty, if you want to put it that way, will always override personal feeling should you come upon a fellow Jew in distress. The sorts of institutions mentioned above excited the envy and admiration even of medieval Christians, hardly a Jew-loving bunch, to the point where "if the Jews can do it, why can't we" became a common literary motif. The fourteenth-century English poet William Langland expresses this sentiment in *Piers Plowman*, one of the seminal works of Middle English literature:

A Iew wolde noght se a Iew go Ianglyng for defaute
For alle the mebles on this moolde, and he amende it
    myghte.

Allas that a cristene creature shal be unkynde til another!
Syn Iewes, that we Iugge Iudas felawes,
Eyther of hem helpeth oother of that that hym nedeth,
Whi ne wol we cristene of cristes good be as kynde?
So Iewes shul ben oure loresmen, shame to us alle!

[A Jew would not see a Jew crying out for want
For all the goods in this world, if he could do anything
    about it.
Alas that one Christian creature should be unkind to
    another!
Since Jews, whom we consider the confederates of
    Judas—
Each of them helps the other with that which he needs,
Why are we Christians not as liberal with Christ's goods?
Shame on all of us, that Jews should be our teachers.]

A society of this type demands that its members learn to put the interests of the community as a whole ahead of their private preferences and demands; if you can't see why someone else's desires might be more important than your own or why the needs of the community subsume and surpass those of any particular member, then you become a liability, no matter how much you might otherwise have to offer.

On the other hand, your willingness to help look out for others means that they will help look out for you. One of the standard questions in ethics courses when I was in university had to do with a man whose wife was desperately ill. The drugs that would cure her cost far more than the man was able to afford, and the local pharmacist was unwilling to arrange a schedule of graduated payments or give him a deal on the price. The question was: Is the man justified in breaking into the pharmacy and stealing the drugs? Is this right, or should he stand helplessly by while his wife dies of her disease?

This is not a Jewish question. In the kind of community we're talking about, the husband would go to the sick benefit or free loan society in his town (or in the closest one large enough to have one); he could appeal to the local rabbi or rabbis either for help with raising funds or, if the druggist was Jewish, for applying moral and community pressure on the druggist, who, if nothing else, might have children whom he'd like to see married one day. If the cost was too great for the local community and the druggist wasn't Jewish, recourse, often through rabbinic intervention, might be had to similar organizations in larger towns and cities, philanthropists, or—more commonly— druggists elsewhere who might offer a better price.

So deeply ingrained was the idea of relying on these institutions that one-stop, geographically based versions of them were among the earliest organizations founded by East European Jewish immigrants in America. Some of these *landsmanshaften* or "societies of compatriots" still exist; just take a look at the section names in any large Jewish cemetery. After World War II, these *landsmanshaften* also undertook the publication of memorial books for the Jewish communities of the now Jewless towns whose names they bear. Class-conscious versions of these locally based organizations—workers' benevolent and mutual aid societies—played a significant role in the American labor movement; the socialists, the Orthodox, and the indifferent were all still thinking Jewish.

The *landsmanshaften* can help clarify the earlier metaphor of the sandlot ball game. Imagine that you're on your way to the library to study for an exam that you'll be writing in two weeks' time. As you're walking by the *landsmanshaft*, though, one of the nine people inside calls you over and explains that they need a tenth for a minyan, and since you seem to know what he's talking about, it's going to be you. You protest: you've got an exam, you don't come from that town, neither did your parents or grandparents; you're a girl (this would have worked until fairly recently), you're not a girl, whatever, but all to no avail. You have no choice and you end up having to go inside for anywhere between fifteen and forty-five minutes, depending on the time of day. Afterward, they offer you a shot of whiskey and wish you luck on the exam.

This is Judaism in action. If the exam was about to begin, they'd look for someone else, after detaining you just long enough to make sure that someone else comes along. Otherwise, though, there is no choice involved; the commonweal always comes first and you go in whether you feel like it or not. Refusal to participate in a minyan—where your grudging attendance is all that's really needed—is taken as a nonverbal way of saying, "Go fuck yourself." The day will probably come when you need nine other people to help you say Kaddish, and you, too, will have to depend, not on the kindness of strangers, but on their sense of reciprocal obligation. That's why the Talmud says *all* Israel are responsible for each other: not only a certain class, not just the good ones, but everybody without exception.

VI

THE OBVERSE OF this approach to life, the other side of the coin, is that everybody becomes responsible for anybody's sins. This is a problem faced by all minorities; if just one of their members does something stupid or vicious, the victims and witnesses and people who hear about it are liable to decide that such behavior is typical of the whole group. In light of the traditional Jewish view that the Children of Israel are supposed to behave in a way that does credit to their Creator, it shouldn't come as much of a surprise to discover that Judaism refers to such behavior, the kind that makes a whole people look bad, as *khilel ha-shem*, "defamation or desecration of the name of God." The idea is that non-Jews will take a look at someone like Jack Abramoff or the Rubashkin family of Postville, Iowa— flamboyantly Jewish people guilty of breaching the most fundamental laws of human decency—and conclude that they are the logical outcome of the Jewish way of life and belief.

Such Orthodox malefactors provide us with a fine example of what can happen when a culture loses touch with itself, when it forgets why it is doing the things that it does. All you have to do is open a Bible to see that the Jewish legal system consists to a large degree of a series of often incomprehensible prohibitions. As Maimonides, paraphrasing a Talmudic exposition of the same idea (*Yoma* 67a), explained almost a thousand years ago, there are two types of commandments:

> *Mishpotim*, ordinances, are commandments with reasons
> that are obvious and benefits that are immediately ap-

parent, such as the prohibitions against theft and blood-shed and the obligation to honor one's father and mother. *Khukim*, decrees, are commandments without any clear reason. Our sages said: "I [God] have decreed these things for you and you have no authorization to enquire into the reasons for them." Our evil inclinations kick against them and the nations of the world try to gainsay them: for example, the prohibitions against pork or eating meat with dairy and the commandments concerning the cow with the broken neck and the red heifer and the scapegoat.

(MISHNEH TORAH, *Laws Concerning the Misuse of Sacramental Objects* 8:8)

These commandments—which don't really affect an omnipotent and omniscient deity one way or the other—offer us a sort of training in the control and redirection of our impulses and desires. They teach us how to think of others just as soon as we think of ourselves. Remember what Rabbi Elazar said: "I really want to eat pork and sleep with Moabite showgirls, *but* . . ." There are no brownie points for someone who says "*feh*" to roast suckling pig and makes barf noises when entering a gentlemen's club; you might just as well refrain from murder because the sight of a corpse makes you faint. The point behind not doing what you want to do has to be that you *want* to do it; when you don't do what you want to do, it isn't because you have suppressed your desire, it is because you have surpassed it:

Rav said: The commandments were given only for the sake of refining humanity. For what does God care if one person slaughters from the front of the animal's neck and another does so from the back? You must admit then that the commandments were given only to refine humanity.

(GENESIS RABBO 44:1)

Done properly, what sets Judaism apart from other systems of belief is the idea that it ain't what you don't do, it's the way you don't do it. If you didn't do it but think you did, you're as guilty, morally, as if you'd done it:

When Rabbi Chiya bar Ashi's wife overheard him praying to be delivered from sexual temptation, she said, "Why is he saying such a thing when he's been too old for us to have relations for years now?" One day when he was studying in his garden, she fixed herself up, changed her clothes, and walked back and forth in front of him a couple of times. "Who are you?" he asked. "I am Khoru-soh [a famous prostitute] and I'm on my way home from work." He asked her for sex. She said, "I'll take the pomegranate that's on the little branch on the top of that tree as payment." He leapt up, got to the top of the tree, and gave it to her.

When he came home, his wife was heating the oven. He got inside. "What are you doing?" she asked. He told her what had happened, and she said, "That was me." He paid her no mind until she showed him the pomegranate. He said, "Nevertheless, I intended to do something forbidden." Rabbi Chiya suffered over this for the rest of his life until it finally killed him.

(KIDDUSHIN 81B)

While this is the real, acted-out version of the sin that Jesus called "adultery . . . in his heart" and that got Jimmy Carter into so much trouble when he ran for president, it is also the plot of many a comedy and could be looked on as a sort of proto–Woody Allen script. Not only does Rabbi Chiya never seem to notice any resemblance between his wife and the best-known hooker in town, but the old man's leap to the top of the tree and subsequent hop into the oven are rife with cinematic possibility.

The point, though, is that as far as Chiya is concerned, he cheated and got caught, even if the woman *with* whom he cheated was also the woman *on* whom he cheated. He intended to deceive his wife; he thought he'd deceived his wife; and the fact that it was his wife all along merely added an extra element of shame to his already powerful feelings of guilt. As Rabbi Akiva says on the very same page:

> What happens if someone is planning to eat pork but ends up eating mutton instead? The Torah tells us that he must atone and be forgiven. How much the more so then if he's planning to eat pork and actually does so?
>
> (KIDDUSHIN 81B)

While the intent to do what is right does not justify a bad or evil act, the intent to do wrong deprives an otherwise laudable action of any real moral value. If you smuggle a starving child out of Darfur, you're a *mentsh*—and then some; if you find the same child hiding in your trunk after you land in Cairo, the kid's no less alive, but has managed to preserve herself without any effort on your part. Saving someone from getting onto a train that neither of you knows is about to explode is simple happenstance; if he misses that train because you're busy robbing him, you're still a *gonif*, and asking the judge for clemency because you ended up saving the victim's life is nothing but chutzpah.

Classical Jewish thought stands in categorical opposition to the idea that good ends can justify not-so-good means. "A good deed leads to a good deed, a transgression to a transgression," the Mishna tells us (*Ovos* 4:2); you don't embezzle money to give yourself time to study Torah. Conversely, you don't use the study of Torah or any other aspect of traditional Jewish learning or life to justify your own prejudices, stupidity, or refusal to follow the dictates of common sense. You're not supposed to, at any rate. The Talmud provides two direct illustrations of the sort of person who does so:

> A foolish hasid [i.e., a *shmuck* who uses religion to justify his *shmuckishness*] is like what? It's like he's walking and there's a woman drowning in the river and he says, "It's not right for me to look at her in order to save her."
>
> (SOTAH 21B)

> He sees a child thrashing about in the river and says, "I'll take off my phylacteries and save him," except that by the time he gets the phylacteries off, the child has died.
>
> (YERUSHALMI SOTAH 4:1)

The Yiddish word for this particular type of *shmuck* is *khnyok*. Defined by Weinreich as "bigot, philistine; petty, unreasonable conservative," a *khnyok* can also be characterized as a *shmuck* with a rule book, the sanctimonious type who is ready to find fault with everybody for not living up to the standards that she has taken it upon herself to enforce. The zealots and ideologues mentioned earlier would all be called *khnyoks* in Yiddish.

The Talmud makes no bones about the consequences of *khnyokish* behavior. In explaining why Jerusalem was destroyed, the rabbis tell the story of how a man named Bar Kamtso tried to frame the whole Jewish people by telling the Roman emperor that the Jews would refuse to offer the emperor's sacrifice in the Temple. When the emperor sends a calf to Jerusalem to be sacrificed, Bar Kamtso makes a blemish in its upper lip. Such a blemish disqualified an animal from being offered in the Temple:

> The rabbis considered offering it to avoid trouble with the government when Rabbi Zechariah ben Avkilos said, "People will say that we offer animals with blemishes on the altar."
>
> They then considered killing Bar Kamtso to keep him from informing on them, but Rabbi Zechariah said, "They'll say that we killed him for making a blemish in a sacrificial animal."
>
> Rabbi Yochanan said, "The humility of Rabbi Zechariah ben Avkilos destroyed our Temple and burnt our Sanctuary and caused us to be exiled from our land."
>
> (GITIN 56A)

As neither *shmuck* nor *khnyok* would be coined for more than another millennium, the Talmud was forced to talk about

Zechariah ben Avkilos's "humility," that is, his fear of what others might think, of how those not in full possession of the facts might misinterpret the proper course of action and possibly cause him to lose face before his inferiors. Zechariah's "humility" is usually interpreted as lack of understanding. He is so concerned with appearing to obey the law that his action—or nonaction—finally makes its continued fulfillment impossible. This truly insane hyperliteral approach makes Zechariah the Inspector Javert of Jewish law; what it makes of the rabbis who didn't reject his suicidal plan out of hand is another question entirely.

VII

ZECHARIAH BEN AVKILOS lets us see what happens when we fulfill any kind of ethical or ceremonial requirements solely for the sake of discharging them or showing others how much closer we stand to heaven and The Big Fellow Who Lives There than they do. Subtle and even profound ideas undergo a process of *shmuckification* that turns them into parodies of their original intent. They become sticks with which to beat the less punctilious, mirrored sticks into which the beaters can gaze upon the glory of their own righteousness—regardless of the price exacted thereby from the community as a whole.

Yet people like Zechariah or the anonymous but foolish hasidim described in the Talmud are no less slovenly or self-indulgent than the beer-sodden *zhlob* of whom they would most certainly disapprove, the kind of guy who takes his eyes off the TV only to avoid stepping on his kids on his way to the fridge. Zechariah, the foolish hasid, and the drunk have all given in to their basest impulses. They might have started from different bases, but they all share the same feeling of self-satisfaction. The guy with the beer is unquestionably the least dangerous of the bunch; the hasid puts paid to the odd individual life; and Zechariah ben Avkilos causes the destruction of an entire civilization. To use mitzvahs for your own advantage—even if the advantage is only a deep feeling of self-pride—is to turn them into transgressions, which produce nothing but further transgressions, further instances of wrongdoing.

The Talmud goes on to detail the consequences of Zechariah ben Avkilos's disastrous scruples. In discussing the siege of Jerusalem, the rabbis explain how three men of extraordinary wealth pledge enough necessities to keep the city going for the next twenty-one years. The local zealots, who want to fight the Romans rather than make peace, burn the storehouses and deliberately bring about a famine; Rabbi Yochanan ben Zakkai manages to sneak out of the city and get an audience with the emperor, who agrees to grant any request that he might make. And what does Rabbi Yochanan ask for? The same old roll with butter that we saw with Bontshe Shvayg. "Give me [the town of] Yavne and its wise men [i.e., the Sanhedrin]," he says, "and the dynasty of Rabban Gamaliel and doctors to cure Rabbi Zadok." And the rest of 'em can all go to hell.

Imagine that Hugo Chávez has used his petrodollars to buy the whole of the United States, except for New York, which he has placed under siege. A well-known public intellectual smuggles himself out of the city and gets to Chávez, who agrees to grant him a boon. Instead of asking for New York, the public figure says: "Give me New Haven and its sages; the Kennedys, including Arnold Schwarzenegger; and a cardiologist to look after Dick Cheney." A grateful America would most surely salute:

> Rabbi Joseph or Rabbi Akiva said, "[God] turns wise men back and makes their knowledge into foolishness" (Isa. 44:25). Yochanan should have said, "Let them [Jerusalem and its people] off this time." But he didn't think that he would be granted so much and that if he were to ask for it, not even a little would be saved.
>
> (GITIN 56B)

Yochanan's "Give me Yavne" should have been preceded by "If you won't give me Jerusalem." While it is entirely possible that the Vespasian of the Talmud (who shouldn't be identified too closely with the Vespasian of history) would never have given Yochanan all of Jerusalem and its inhabitants, Yochanan had a duty to ask for it. His instinctively narrow focus on himself and his colleagues looks even worse when compared with the bargaining that Abraham engages in to try to save Sodom from the wrath of God—who's supposed to be a lot scarier and more powerful than any emperor—in the eighteenth chapter of Genesis. Abraham takes his life in his hands by asking, and he does so five times. Zechariah ben Avkilos and Yochanan ben Zakkai are too self-absorbed to do anything but give up before they've even tried: each is willing to sacrifice the general welfare to the interests of his own reputation or friends or idée fixe. As the Talmud tells us further:

> [Simeon bar Yochai and his son] had been hiding in a cave for twelve years when Elijah the prophet appeared at its

opening and said, "Has no one let Bar Yochai know that the emperor has died and that his death sentence against Bar Yochai has been annulled?" They went out and saw that people were plowing and sowing, and Bar Yochai said, "They forsake the eternal life and occupy themselves with a transitory life," and every place on which he and his son cast their eyes burst into flame immediately. A voice came out of heaven and said, "Did you come out of there to destroy my world? Get back in your cave."

(SHABBOS 33B)

[When they came out again twelve months later, they had learned their lesson.]

These people aren't really wicked; they're much more dangerous than that. The wicked can be brought to judgment and punished; these others continue to refract everything through their own desires and are unable to see clearly once their immediate interests come into play—which is, regrettably, always. They're *shmucks*, well-meaning *shmucks* who might just as well be wicked for all the good that they do.

THREE

Extending the *Shmuck*

I

THE TALMUD AND the rabbinic literature associated with it have a great deal to say about the kind of *shmucks* whose own interests are their only interest. The Mishna, the earlier part of the Talmud, completed around the year 200 but drawing on much older material, gives quite a detailed portrait of the kind of person whom we would call a *shmuck*. The term that the Mishna uses is "golem." While science-fiction and fantasy fans are familiar with the golem as a proto-robot, the rabbinically animated forerunner of Frankenstein's monster, the word did not acquire this meaning until relatively late in its history. *Golem* started out as something considerably different.

The word is first found in the Bible, where it occurs in Psalm 139, verse 16: "Your eyes saw my golem." The Revised Standard Version translates *golem* as "unformed substance";

the Jewish Publication Society Bible has "unformed limbs";
the idea of formlessness or lack of definition is paramount, and
harks all the way back to the primal matter at the beginning of
Genesis, where the earth is without form and void. This idea of
something raw, unfinished, undifferentiated becomes the chief
meaning of the word in ancient postbiblical writings. According to the Talmud:

> The day [of Adam's creation] lasted twelve hours. In the
> first hour, his dust was gathered together; in the second, he
> became a golem; in the third, his limbs were stretched out;
> in the fourth, his soul was tossed into him.
>
> (SANHEDRIN 38B)

The golem here is a featureless lump with no identifiable
characteristics whatever, not even limbs. More important,
though, it has yet to acquire a soul. A golem has all the material that goes into a human being, but it still needs work, plenty
of shaping and polishing, along with actual animation, before
it will come to resemble something that we might think of as
human. A golem is to a man or woman as a chunk of dough is
to a loaf of bread; indeed, a related rabbinic tradition (*Genesis
Rabbo* 8:1) describes how the raw material of Adam-the-golem
was stretched from one end of the world to the other, as if pri-
mordial man were really a primal pizza.

It is this idea of incompletion that causes the legendary au-
tomaton to be called a golem. A golem can do anything that a
person can do—stories of people using golems as unsalaried
butlers are legion—except think and speak, the two activities
that separate human beings from everything else. If you tell a

golem to do something, it will keep doing it until you give it an explicit command to stop. If you ask a golem a question, it will stare at you and say nothing. Hence the colloquial use of golem in Yiddish to denote a slow-moving, ungainly, dull-witted sort of person; *zitsn vi a leymener goylem*, "to sit like a golem made of clay," is to be the Yiddish equivalent of a cigar store Indian, someone who just sits there, silent and immobile. You talk and talk, ask questions, try to draw her out, but not a word comes out of her mouth and you begin to wonder if she's really human or merely a clever simulation. The golem—the real one, that is—has the outward physical features of a human being, but is like Adam in the third hour of creation: it has arms and legs, but lacks brain and soul. It is a rough draft of a human being, basic material still sorely in need of refinement.

It can hardly be an accident, then, that the Mishna chooses the word *golem*, rather than something that means "fool" or "unlearned person," to describe the opposite of a sage or wise man. But typically for a document that has had so much influence on Yiddish patterns of thought and speech, the Mishna only mentions things that the golem *doesn't* do. These are:

- Keep silent in the face of someone with more experience and education.
- Let a person finish speaking without interrupting him.
- Consider what he's going to say before making any reply.
- Confine his questions to the matter under discussion and give direct answers to any questions that he's asked.
- Address matters in the order in which they've been presented.

- Say "I didn't hear you," when he doesn't hear [i.e., admit to not understanding what has been said].
- And admit the truth when he is found to have erred.

(OVOS 5:7)

In other words, a golem is the kind of person who knows more about everything than you do and never shuts up about it. He doesn't listen to what you're saying because he's too busy talking at the same time, jumps from one topic to another with no rhyme or reason, and refuses to acknowledge any fact that could indicate that he isn't right. As the technology necessary for radio or television news-talk shows had not been developed at the time of the Mishna, these were still unambiguously negative characteristics. In a culture that valued debate above almost all other human activity, the inability to converse properly disqualified a person from full participation in society. Look up the word *conversation* in any English dictionary and you'll see that it comes from the Latin *conversari*, which doesn't mean "to talk," but "to live with, keep company with." Someone who doesn't know how to talk to other human beings doesn't know how to live with other human beings; the Mishna might call him a golem, but he's really a *shmuck* in a toga. Remember Mr. Cohen, the "cancer, shmancer" guy from chapter 1? Just move him back a couple of thousand years and you'll see that the golem is like the synagogue on the other side of the road from yours: he is the person you *don't* talk to. But that doesn't always mean that he isn't talking to you already.

In his commentary on this Mishnaic passage, Moses Maimonides, the incredibly influential twelfth-century rabbi and philosopher whose fans included Saint Thomas Aquinas, elaborates on the difference between the golem and everyone else:

> A golem is a person who possesses some intellectual and moral virtues, but without any of them being complete or properly ordered. They are confused and mixed up and contaminated with defects. [Such a person is called a golem] because of his resemblance to productions of an artisan which have received their basic shape but have not been refined and finished, like a knife or sword that the smith has not finished: they have only their most basic form, but have yet to be whetted and sharpened and polished.
>
> (COMMENTARY ON *Ovos* 5:7)

Maimonides bases his interpretation on the relatively common Mishnaic use of *golem* to mean "unfinished vessel or utensil, artisanal production still in progress." The golem that he describes has failed to reach at least one essential stage of human development; just as a spoon that needs planing and buffing is still unfit for use, though it has the form and appearance of a spoon, so the golem falls a step or so short of real *mentsh*-hood. He has a body, but still needs "to be whetted and sharpened and polished" before he can be anything other than a walking *klots*—that's klutz in English—a great big chunk of wood that lies athwart the path to social relations.

The wise person with whom the Mishna contrasts the golem is not described as clever or well informed, but only as knowing how to make his or her conversation an orderly thing that takes account of the presence and feelings of the other party. The Mishnaic golem differs from the robo-golem of more recent times in that he's the unquestioning servant of his own desires, rather than someone else's. The human golem can talk, but not converse; he can holler, and is more interested in shutting you up than hearing you out. Male or female, the golem is not a complete *mentsh*—not yet, at any rate—but is still an unfinished part-*mentsh*. The Yiddish folk-mind has narrowed him down to a very specific part, the one least inclined to submit to instruction or accept limitation and most likely to do whatever it feels like doing. Imagine human character as an erection-in-waiting—when it isn't bouncing back and forth, flaccid and absurd, it is hard, dumb, and tough to control—and you'll know exactly what we're dealing with.

II

RICK WILCOX, ONE of the leading figures in contemporary American mountaineering, discovered an unusually clear case of the kind of human underdevelopment that we're talking about. There's no better example of a clueless golem or a *shmuck* in motion than the high-altitude specimen that Wilcox ran across in the Himalayas a number of years ago. Discovering a fellow climber in life-threatening distress, Wilcox and his wife arranged for a helicopter to get the climber out of danger and off the mountain. They were more than a little taken aback when the person whose life they'd saved "stiffed us," as Wilcox put it, "for the helicopter bill."

If *shmucks* had legs, this guy would be Bigfoot. The willingness to accept help, as if having his life saved were his due; the self-importance that leads him to think that a total stranger should be happy to foot the bill; the dishonesty, ingratitude, chutzpah, and lack of manners, not to mention the complete absence of any scruple about repaying good—genuine, altruistic, nothing-in-it-for-the-benefactor good—not with evil, so much as with contempt, brings us about as close to *shmuckish* perfection as we're likely to get. This is a guy who can't converse; his only problem with other people is that they exist when he has no use for them. It's one thing to cheat the reaper, it's something else to cheat the guy who cheated him for you. All that's missing is a lawsuit against Wilcox, ideally for having come between the plaintiff and his original plans.

While this alpine asshole might have reached the summit of recent *shmuckishness* and set a benchmark for the entire twenty-first century, he can't be said to have done so alone. Today's *shmucks* have a lengthy pedigree behind them, extending in mythological terms all the way back to the beginning of time. We can witness the birth of the *shmuck* near the opening of the book of Genesis, the chronology of which seems to imply that even before there were people, there were *shmucks*.

Full as it is of sinners, evildoers, and deeply flawed heroes, the Hebrew Bible is a virtual encyclopedia of *shmuckish* activity from its earliest pages on. Adam and Eve start to behave like *shmucks* only a few short lines after they have both been created. While the Christian notion of original sin doesn't jibe very well with standard Jewish ways of thought, the idea that, left to his own devices, an untutored human being stands a better than even chance of turning into a *shmuck* most assuredly does: all he has to do is talk to another person. The story of the Tree of Knowledge and the expulsion from Eden can be read as the overture to a still unfinished symphony of *shmuckishness*.

If there's a mythological element to any of this, something that might strike a thoroughgoing rationalist as hard to believe, it is only that it is possible to be a *shmuck* without even being human. Adam and Eve have been created at the end of the second chapter of Genesis; the first line of chapter 3 states that "the snake was the most cunning of all the beasts of the field that the Lord had made." The Hebrew word translated as "cunning," *arum*, looks the same as the Hebrew word for "naked." In the verse immediately before this one, Adam and Eve are described as *arumim* (that's the plural adjective), "naked, unconcealed, open," and Eve takes the serpent's leading question—"Did God actually tell you not to eat from any tree in the garden?" (Gen. 3:1)—as an open, honest inquiry with no ulterior motive behind it.

Now, the serpent himself is quite a *shmuck*, the kind who can't stand to see others enjoying themselves. Rashi, whom we met in the last chapter, says, "The snake saw them naked, having sex where all could see, and he lusted for Eve." Rashi's commentary is printed alongside Scripture itself in all traditional editions of the Hebrew Bible, and this particular passage was once known to virtually every Jewish schoolchild. I'm not going to linger on the phallic associations of the snake and their peculiar appropriateness to a discussion of *shmek*—the English "shlong" for penis comes from the Yiddish *shlang*, which has a clean meaning of "snake" and a dirty one of *shmuck*, in the anatomical sense—except to note that when schoolkids used to translate Rashi's comments from Hebrew to Yiddish, the idea of a *shlang* seeing two people having sex and wanting a bit for itself produced plenty of schoolboy quips and giggles, pre-Freud as well as post-, especially in view of the fact that Rashi prefaces the above remarks by discussing "why the snake came to Eve," rather than Adam. This would have been translated as *far vos* the *shlang* came to the woman, which could be taken as a lesson in biology just as easily as in "what brought death into the world and all our woe." Human history begins on a bad night in an interspecies singles bar.

The snake's conversation with Eve is not only a fairly intense version of aggressive bar talk, it is also presented as the first conversation ever to take place between any of God's creatures. The snake's opening gambit is a classic example of what biblical and rabbinic tradition call "wronging" or "cheating" or "fraud" in speech: neither party to the conversation tells the truth, and each is lying in order to get their own way. The Talmud explains the idea of cheating in speech:

What does it mean when Scripture says, "Do not wrong one another" (Lev. 25:17)? It refers to wronging in speech. If someone is a penitent, do not say to him, "Remember your former deeds." If he is the child of converts, do not say, "Remember what your parents did." If he is a convert himself and comes to study Torah, do not say, "Can a mouth that has eaten cadavers and carrion, abominable, creeping things, come to learn the Torah that came forth from the mouth of the Almighty?" If someone is afflicted, if he is visited with illnesses or has buried his children, do not speak to him as Job's friends did: "Is your fear of God not your confidence? Isn't the integrity of your ways your hope? Recall, has an innocent person ever perished?" (Job 4:6–7). If donkey drivers come seeking grain, do not say, "Go to X, who is a grain merchant," when you know well that X has never been in that business. Rabbi Judah said, "Do not pretend to be interested in making a purchase when you have no money, for this is something that is concealed in your heart, and with respect to things that are a matter of the heart, it is written 'and you shall fear your God'" (Lev. 25:17).

(BOVO METSIYO 58B)

The snake tricks Eve by asking a leading question disguised as an exercise in information gathering, but before she becomes the first poor *shmuck* in the world, the credulous dupe who ends up suffering because she's bought a bill of goods, Eve unwittingly helps the serpent along. She tells him that God has commanded her and Adam "not to eat of it [the tree] or touch it, lest [they] die" (Gen. 3:3). God said nothing about touching, only eating; Eve's attempt to go one step beyond the commandment, to make the prohibition more stringent than it was—to be more religious than God, as it were—becomes the efficient cause of her downfall. Rashi tells us that "the snake pushed her into the tree and said, 'Just as touching it didn't kill you, neither will eating from it.'" As the Jerusalem Talmud asks in a slightly different context: "What the law has forbidden isn't enough for you? You've got to go and forbid yourself other things, too?" (*Yerushalmi Nedorim* 9:1).

Well before Rashi, the Midrash seized upon Eve's unwarranted "touch" to comment: "Don't make the fence any bigger than it needs to be, lest it fall over and destroy the plants [that it's supposed to be protecting]" (*Genesis Rabbo* 19:3). By adding what she probably thought of as insurance, all Eve managed to do was give the *shlang* yet another opening to screw her. As Rashi says, "The snake's words made sense to her. They pleased her and she believed them"; believed them because she *wanted* to believe them, because they seemed to be in line with what she already wanted.

The serpent is a *shmuck* in the sense of being gratuitously mean or nasty. He knows full well the consequences of eating from the tree, but hopes that once Eve's eyes have been opened, she'll give him a tumble, either out of gratitude or because she's finally noticed his natural charm. For the sake of a little snake-on-lady action, he is willing to risk the future of everything on earth.

Eve falls under the heading of one who is "gullible, easily duped, naive," but not without a powerful belief in her own intelligence. She is the first person to engage in one of the most quintessentially *shmucky* of activities: thinking herself clever while behaving like a complete screaming fool. Adding a needless and dangerous prohibition is only the first mistake she makes. Rashi asks why she gave the fruit to her husband after she had eaten from the tree. Why risk his anger or sacrifice the intellectual advantage that she had just gained from eating the fruit? Because, he says, she was afraid that "if she died [from eating the fruit] and he were to remain alive, he would marry somebody else." Better he should die, then. No one but the two of them anywhere on earth, and already she's jealous.

It doesn't end there, of course, because Adam also eats the fruit, and when God asks him if he has eaten from the forbidden tree, Adam doesn't bother with a proper answer. "The woman that you put with me gave me," he says (Gen. 3:12), and "you" should be printed in italics: "*You* gave her to me; she made me do it and *you* made her make me, Mr. Omnipotent.

So it isn't my fault, it's *your* fault." Rashi, echoing the Talmud (*Avodo Zoro* 5b), says: "Here he denies the kindness" that God had done him by giving him a companion. It isn't so much the ingratitude itself but the refusal to accept any responsibility for his own actions that makes Adam such a *shmuck* here. He's quite content to land Eve in more trouble, as long as he can get himself off the hook.

Not a terribly auspicious start for human life, and things get worse as early as the beginning of the next chapter, when Cain and Abel prove that the fruit, if you'll pardon the expression, doesn't fall too far from the tree. While the Bible has Cain kill Abel because he is jealous that God preferred Abel's sacrifice to his own, there is a tradition that links their rivalry a little more closely with the character traits already demonstrated by their mother. According to the Midrash, the two boys divided the world up between themselves, then argued over whose half the Temple was going to be in. The Middle East hasn't changed since the beginning of time; the story of Cain and Abel constitutes the first case of the kind of *shmuckery* in the name of God that has come to define so much of our world today.

Fraternal jealousy comes up again near the end of Genesis in the story of Joseph and his brothers. The latter respond to their father's unconcealed partiality to Joseph and Joseph's unquestionably obnoxious behavior (excused somewhat by his being a spoiled teenager; his brothers are all grown men) by selling him into slavery instead of going through with their original plan of murdering him. They then tell Jacob, their father, that Joseph was torn apart by a wild beast. Jacob's reaction? "He refused to be comforted" (Gen. 37:35). His sons' reaction is not recorded. Three chapters earlier, two of these brothers, Levi and

Simeon, massacre a city. In the chapter following that, Reuben, the eldest, beds his father's concubine (who is also the mother of two of his brothers). In the chapter that follows the story of Joseph, Judah, another of the brothers, is about to burn his daughter-in-law at the stake for adultery until she proves that her sin, unlike Adam's, really is someone else's fault and that someone else is Judah. Whatever else they might have been, the sons of Jacob certainly seem to constitute the earliest fraternity of *shmek* on record.

The Bible goes on to detail some really first-rate instances of *shmuckishness*—the Children of Israel kvetching their way out of Egypt and through forty years in the desert; their worship of the Golden Calf while Moses is still on the mountain receiving the Tablets of the Law; much of the politics in the courts of David and Solomon, or the prophet Elisha having forty-two children mangled by she-bears for calling him "baldy"—but the climax, the apogee of paleo-*shmuckery* (it's like the *paleo* in paleontology, from the Greek for "ancient") is the tale of Kamtso and Bar Kamtso that forms the backdrop to the story of Zechariah ben Avkilos that we looked at in the last chapter. Since we already know where the story is going, we will be able to see quite clearly how a single stupid act started a snowball of *shmuckery* that brought about the destruction of the Second Temple. The Talmud tells us:

> Jerusalem was destroyed because of Kamtso and Bar Kamtso. A man who was a friend of Kamtso and an enemy of Bar Kamtso once gave a party and told his servant, "Go bring me Kamtso"; he went and brought him Bar Kamtso.
>
> (GITIN 55B)

Kamtso means "locust," Bar Kamtso, "the son of a locust" or "locust, junior"; it is doubtful that these were anybody's real names. The Talmud is trying to tell us that an entire civilization can fall over something as trivial as a "bar" before the name of an otherwise undistinguished person; over Joe McShmo receiving an invitation that was supposed to have gone to Joe Shmo. Raw human nature will do all the rest:

> When the host found Bar Kamtso sitting there he said, "You are my enemy; what do you want here? Get up and get out."
>
> Bar Kamtso said, "Since I'm here already, let me stay and I'll pay you for what I eat and drink."
>
> "No," said his host.
>
> "I'll pay for half the party."
>
> "No."
>
> "Then I'll pay for the whole party."
>
> "No," and he took Bar Kamtso by the hand, drew him up, and took him out.
>
> (GITIN 55B–56A)

It was hardly Bar Kamtso's fault that he was invited to the party in error; as he was the host's enemy, he would not have recognized the servant who came to fetch him and who does not seem to have mentioned who was holding the party. Once the host has realized the mistake, he chooses to follow his dislike rather than the trail of error. Instead of shrugging his shoulders or getting mad at the servant, he chooses to shame the innocent Bar Kamtso, who seems desperate to avoid the ignominy of being thrown out of the party in front of a roomful

of people. By offering to pay the whole bill, he is not only willing to make sure that the party-thrower loses nothing by allow-
ing him to stay, but effectively provides him with the means to
have another party to which he—Bar Kamtso—will assuredly
not be invited. But the host has clearly worked himself into a
state of some dudgeon about Bar Kamtso's chutzpah in turning
up in the first place; he's too busy savoring his hatred, is too
much of a *shmuck* to be able to see Bar Kamtso's point of view,
and has him thrown out anyway.

> Bar Kamtso said, "Since the rabbis who were sitting there
> did not protest, that must show that they approve [of the
> host's behavior], so I will go and chew things over with
> [inform on them to] the government."
>
> (GITIN 56A)

The rabbis' silence suggests that the scene has played out
loudly and publicly, rather than in discreet undertones. Bar
Kamtso's assumption that their inaction indicates acquies-
cence—or perhaps only indifference—becomes a lot more
credible when we see how ready they are to act when he brings
the blemished calf to the Temple. Indeed, Samuel Eidels, known
as the Maharsho (died 1631), one of the most eminent and influential of Talmudic commentators, asks why the rabbis kept
silent:

> You could say that perhaps they failed to protest because
> they were unable to do so, and perhaps this was so because
> of the sycophancy that prevailed in that generation.
>
> (MAHARSHO *to Gitin* 56A)

They were afraid to speak out in front of the wealthy and well-connected party-thrower, who was in a position to be able to do them harm, and they let their fear come between them and their duty, just as they later allowed Zechariah ben Avkilos and his noticeably warped logic to lead them to certain destruction. Zechariah is a total Talmudic nobody who is mentioned on only one other occasion (*Shabbos* 143a), but the Midrash gives us reason to believe that he had plenty of *shlep*, and that the host of the party would have paid attention had he spoken: "Zechariah ben Avkilos was there [at the party]; *he* was able to protest, but did not do so" (*Eikho Rabbo* 4:3, my emphasis). The Midrash makes Bar Kamtso a lot more subtle than he is in the Talmud.

Angry as Bar Kamtso is, it is almost inevitable that he decides to act like a *shmuck* in return. Getting back at the discourteous host—treating a *shmuck* like a *shmuck*—isn't enough for him, though. If Bar Kamtso had expected (or received) different treatment, he and the host might not have been enemies in the first place. Bar Kamtso is after the rabbinic establishment that allows *shmek* like the host to corrupt it for their own ends. If we follow the Midrash, we can also say that he knew that Zechariah ben Avkilos would end up making the decision about the sacrifice. Bar Kamtso knew exactly where his vengeance was going to lead.

It isn't that he had no reason to be angry. As Maimonides puts it:

> One should be neither as easily angered as a choleric person nor as impervious to anger as a corpse, but should occupy a middle ground. One should get angry only about some-

thing that is worth getting angry about, in order to keep
such a thing from happening again.

(MISHNEH TORAH, Laws of Conduct 1:4)

Anyone who has grown up in a traditional Jewish home
knows how *much* is worth getting angry about if you're a
parent, but Maimonides counsels temperance; there are few
things that a hissy fit will keep from recurring. The traditional
attitude toward anger is that it is a *shmuckifying* agent par
excellence, capable of turning an otherwise intelligent person
into an utter idiot: "He who grows angry forgets what he already knows and increases stupidity" (*Nedorim* 22b); "Anger
puts an end to wisdom" (*Pesikta Zutrosi, Va-Eyro*); and, most
tellingly in this case, "Because he was swayed by anger, he was
swayed by error" (*Sifre, Matos* 5). By going after the rabbis,
Bar Kamtso is simply repeating the party-thrower's mistake of
placing the blame where it doesn't really belong. This doesn't
let the rabbis off the hook for their indifference, but they're
still not the people who threw him out. Bar Kamtso's anger has
turned him into the image of everything he hates.

There is a well-known Talmudic axiom that holds that
"a person's character is revealed in three things: his cups, his
pocket, and his anger" (*Eruvin* 65b; in Ashkenazic Hebrew,
these three things come out as *be-koyseh, u-bekiseh, u-bekaseh*,
which has a much better beat). You can tell who someone is by
how he behaves when he drinks, how provident and honest he
is in financial matters, and how he acts when angry. Assuming
that Bar Kamtso had had time for a first-century cocktail or two
before being confronted by his host, he acquits himself admira-
bly on the first two scores: he acts politely, makes a reasonable

case for staying, and offers generous compensation for being allowed to do so. But it all goes for naught once he gets angry, and there is nothing that takes a person from *mentsh* to *shmuck* as quickly and as irrevocably as anger.

Since the rabbis at the party, the scholars who are supposed to embody all that is best in the culture, did not come to his defense or object to his ill-treatment, Bar Kamtso decides to take his revenge on the system that makes the rabbis so important:

> He went to the emperor and said, "The Jews have rebelled against you."
>
> "Says who?" asked the emperor.
>
> "Send them a sacrifice and see if they offer it."
>
> He sent a choice calf with Bar Kamtso, who made a blemish in its upper lip . . . a place where we consider it a blemish but they [the gentiles] do not.
>
> (GITIN 56A)

If he, Bar Kamtso, was thrown out of a house on a specious pretext, he was going to make sure that the same thing happened to the rabbis. The Hebrew name of the Temple is *bais ha-mikdosh*, literally, "house of the holy place." Since the days when it was still functioning, it has been known colloquially as *ha-bayis*, "The House," or *bayis sheyni*, "The Second House," to distinguish it from the Temple built by Solomon and destroyed in 586 B.C.E. Bar Kamtso took a legitimate grievance and made it into a rather unfunny joke. Where Bar Kamtso got kicked out of *a* house, he was going to make sure that those who allowed it to happen would be kicked out of *the* house.

Continual upping of the ante in the name of a spurious quid

pro quo or measure for measure has been a leading *shmuckish* characteristic for as long as there have been *shmucks* to overreact. Bar Kamtso, the nobody, the grasshopper's little boy, made sure that no one would ever forget the wrong that he had suffered. If the rabbis raised no protest when an injustice was committed against him, he'd give them an injustice that would open their mouths at last; one way or another, they were going to be screaming. And that's where Zechariah ben Avkilos comes in.

III

WE NEED TO look at one more aspect of the story of Bar Kamtso and the party before we go on to talk about the things that a *mentsh* is supposed to do. *Shmuckish* behavior is usually pretty easy to identify, as long as someone else is engaging in it. Any *shmuck* can get up tomorrow, feeling bad, and say, "I shouldn't have done that; I said the wrong thing; I should have spoken up," and go on with her life. A person who understands *mentsh*-hood will call the aggrieved or offended party and apologize; they will have done the *mentshly* thing and made up, insofar as possible, for having acted like a *shmuck*. The nature of what they did and the nature of the person to whom they did it will determine the future of their relationship, but there's almost sure to be a period of frostiness before relations can return to whatever is normal.

A real *mentsh*, though, will see *shmuckishness* looming, and more often than not—which is the best that we can ever hope for—will know how to avoid it. It's like in old cartoons, when a character steps off the edge of the cliff, pauses for a second, then turns into a lollipop with the word *sucker* on the wrapper in great big letters; a *mentsh* sees the cliff coming up and is smart enough to avoid it. In her mind's eye she envisions a gift-wrapped penis with the word *shmuck* emblazoned on the wrapper and knows what it is that she wants to avoid. This kind of negative visualization—the ability to see what you *don't* want and take steps to prevent it—is one of the cornerstones of *mentsh*-hood, and we're about to see how dire the effects of not practicing it can be. The rabbis' failure to act in the case of Bar Kamtso not only lays the groundwork for all of subsequent Jewish history, it also gives us considerable insight into how a *mentsh* is supposed to behave.

Whoever these people were, however learned they might have been, they were clearly no *mentshn*, and their learning was a sad waste of time. There's an old Hasidic joke about a young man who comes to a famous *rebbe*, a Hasidic leader, and says, "I've been through *gants shas*, the entire Talmud, six times," to which the *rebbe* replies, "And how much of the Talmud has been through you?" No matter what these men knew, it had had no effect on anything but their memories. Their failure to intervene in this instance, their inability to recognize that throwing some nobody out of a party—no matter how big a *makher* the host was—was indeed some skin off their ass, led to the destruction of an entire civilization. They weren't the only guilty parties, but that's what *shmuckery* is like; it's highly, highly contagious.

The violation of *mentsh*-hood committed by the party-giver, the one that the rabbis were so remiss in not protesting, receives more serious treatment in the Talmud than any sin short of murder, despite the fact that this particular transgression is never mentioned directly anywhere in the Bible. It begins with the host's first approach to Bar Kamtso.

The host's treatment of Bar Kamtso begins with verbal disrespect and ends in physical contempt. While no one can force him to like Bar Kamtso any more than Bar Kamtso might like him, they both have a moral obligation to control their feelings and make sure that the strength of their dislike yields to the fact of the other man's humanity. Negative feelings about another person do not make him any less human, no matter how much you might dislike him. "What makes your blood redder than his?" asks the Talmud (*Pesokhim* 25b). What makes you more intrinsically worthy than he is?

You're supposed to back off and "let the honor of your fellow be as dear to you as your own," as the Mishna enjoins, without being quick to anger if he fails to show you the same consideration (*Ovos* 2:10). This is a fancy way of saying, "Other people have the same feelings as you do, and something that would piss you off will probably do the same to them":

> This statement is a first step and support and a remedy to keep a man from becoming angry with his fellow, for his fellow's honor will be as dear to him as his own, in accordance with what is written in Scripture, "And you shall love your neighbor as yourself" (Lev. 19:18). If you hurt your hand, you do not say, "One hand has injured the other, so I'll let the other hand injure this one." . . . If you get angry, it is impossible for you not to affront the honor of your fellow.
>
> (MIDRASH SHMUEL to *Ovos* 2:10)

Loving your neighbor as yourself is the biblical forerunner of all those pop songs in which the singer, to quote Smokey Robinson, tells the sung-to, "I don't like you, but I love you": you don't have to like your neighbor, but you do have to love her, that is, make the same excuses for her and accord her the same consideration as you would for yourself.

Liking is one of those matters of the heart that are always concealed from others, and no moral code or system of ethics can make you like somebody. They can, however, tell you how to act toward people, whether you like them or not. You can treat somebody decently without liking them at all; that's why good manners and courtesy are known in Hebrew as *derekh erets*, literally, "the way of the land"—that's "way" in the sense of "custom"—a term that also covers such activities as earning a living, acquiring the skills by which to do so, and sexual intercourse—all the things that create and sustain a functioning civil society. Interestingly, in Yiddish the same term comes to mean "respect, giving due consideration to the honor of your fellow, loving him as yourself." It's all classed as "the custom of the land" because it's the custom of every land, the only way in which any group of people is able to live together in relative harmony.

You can't be forced to like a person, but you can be prevented from mistreating someone for having a personality or skin color or haircut that might strike you as disagreeable. There is at least an even chance that they feel the same way about you, which is why the Bible makes love the answer. Biblical love, the love decreed in Leviticus, insists that you cut your neighbor the same slack as you cut yourself, that you make as much of an exception of him or her—of everybody, that is—as you're willing to make of yourself; or ideally, as you *would* have made of yourself *if* you happened to be a *shmuck*—which keeps you from holding others to unreasonably high standards.

The verse in which this commandment is found also contains a couple of others: "Do not take vengeance or hold a grudge against your countrymen; you shall love your neighbor as yourself: I am the Lord" (Lev. 19:18). The Talmud defines the difference between taking vengeance and holding a grudge:

> If you say to someone, "Lend me your scythe," and he says, "No," and the next day he says to you, "Lend me your ax," and you say, "You didn't lend to me, so I won't lend to you"—that is vengeance. And what is holding a grudge? You say, "Lend me your ax," and he tells you, "No." The next day he says, "Lend me your garment," and you say, "Here it is. I'm not like you, who wouldn't lend to me." *That* is holding a grudge.
>
> (YOMA 23A)

Simply giving the other person the garment doesn't make you a nice guy; it does not cancel out the hatred that you're nursing in your heart. Essentially, what the Bible is saying is:

- Don't act like a baby.
- Don't conceal hatred and harbor grudges.
- Find the same justifications for people who deal with you as you would find for yourself in dealing with them.
- Try not to hurt them any more than you would try to hurt yourself.

The "I am the Lord" at the end of the verse is God the Father's way of saying, "I really mean it. Don't make me come down there."

In the Talmudic story that we've been looking at, Bar Kamtso asks to be cut some slack by offering to pay for the party, but the host is so intent on keeping his house and his banquet Bar Kamtso–free that he acts as if Bar Kamtso's presence were somehow Bar Kamtso's fault. He tells Bar Kamtso to leave, then lifts him from his seat and throws him out of the house, despite Bar Kamtso's plea for dignity. Indeed, a midrashic version of the same story actually has Bar Kamtso say to the host, "Do not put me to shame, and I will pay for the feast." To which the host replies, "You are not invited" (*Eikho Rabbo* 4:3). The outcome, of course, is exactly the same.

Public humiliation of this type arouses the same horror as murder or idolatry in classic Jewish literature, and strictures against causing embarrassment to others are among the most emphatic in Jewish culture. One person's loss of face can lead to a tit-for-tat cycle of shaming and vengeance that spreads from person to person, community to community, like any other plague, until it infects the whole of society. Because embarrassing someone in public violates a moral, not a penal, code, vengeance is often the only way to punish an offender. We're dealing with a crime that can sidestep any legal system and for which the perpetrator is rarely convicted:

Shaming one's fellow in public is like spilling his blood. Rabbi Nachman bar Yitzchok said: "Well spoken! I have seen the red go out [of a person's face] and the pallor come in."

(BOVO METSIYO 58B)

The idiom translated here as "shaming one's fellow in public" literally means "to whiten his friend's face in public," which makes Rabbi Nachman's comment a lot easier to understand. The idea, of course, is that someone is so mortified by what has been said or done to her that she is quite literally appalled: she turns white, loses something from her face.

Treating people in this way is considered so serious a breach of proper human relations that it is marked out for special treatment in Hell:

> Everyone who goes down to Gehenna comes back up, except for three who descend but do not return. And these are: he who sleeps with another man's wife; he who shames his fellow in public; and he who saddles his fellow with a disparaging nickname.
>
>   Isn't that the same as putting him to shame?
>   They mean even a nickname that he's already used to.
>
>   (BOVO METSIYO 58B)

While the chief Talmudic commentaries seem to be more worried about how long it takes for those who do not reascend to reascend—this is not the typo that it might look like—such concerns do not affect the basic idea that each of these sins involves people who have held others up to mockery, ridicule, or spite, and are unlikely to repent for having done so. These sins are all deeply rooted in the "because I could" way of thinking, the one that we translated a long time ago as "fuck you"; they tend to take something away from the victim without affording the perpetrator any real gain. Neither adultery, face-whitening, or name-calling involves any physical harm; they are ways of undermining the victim's self-image and social standing, and of violating his self-respect, which they can damage or even destroy. Adultery, perhaps surprisingly, is not considered the worst:

> It is better for a man to be suspected of adultery with another man's wife than for him to shame his fellow in public . . . an adulterer is executed by strangulation, but has a portion in the world to come, whereas one who shames his fellow in public has no portion in the world to come.
>
> (BOVO METSIYO 59A; *see also* SANHEDRIN 107A)

> It is better for a person to throw himself into a fiery furnace than to shame his fellow in public. Whence do we know this? From Tamar, as it is written (Gen. 38:25), "When she was brought forth, she sent to her father-in-law."
>
> (BOVO METSIYO 59A)

The idea of flinging yourself into a fiery furnace before shaming someone else in public—even when this someone else might have done something shameful—is mentioned on three other occasions in the Talmud (*Brokhos* 43b; *Kesubos* 67b; *Sotah* 10b), and the story of Judah and Tamar in Genesis 38 is mentioned every time. Tamar was Judah's twice-widowed daughter-in-law. She was married to Judah's son Er, who died without issue, and then to Er's brother, Onan, from whose name we get the term *onanism*; he preferred to spill his seed on the ground rather than inside his wife, lest she bear a son who would be considered the child of his deceased brother. Tamar had waited quite some time for Judah's third son, Shelah, to grow up, so she could marry him, too, but it still hadn't happened. Worried lest she die childless, Tamar disguises herself as a prostitute and sleeps with Judah, who promises to give her a kid as payment. She demands a down payment—who wanders around with a goat under his arm?—and he gives her his seal, its cord, and his staff.

When Tamar, who is still betrothed to Shelah, turns out to be pregnant, she is convicted of adultery (her engagement makes her Shelah's, even before the marriage), and Judah orders her to be burned. As she is about to be consigned to the flames, she says, "I am pregnant by the man to whom these belong. . . . Please acknowledge the owner of this seal and the cords and the staff" (Gen. 38:25). Judah admits his fault and accepts responsibility for the twins that she bears.

Rashi's explanation of this episode reflects the standard view of both the biblical and Talmudic passages:

> She didn't want to shame him by saying, "I am pregnant by you," so instead she said, "the man to whom these belong." She said to herself, "If he admits it on his own, he admits it; if not, let them burn me, but I will not shame him." From here they said, "It is better for a person to throw themselves into a fiery furnace."

Nomads being nomads, Tamar would probably have ended up on a bonfire, but the Talmud's fiery furnace has considerable resonance in Jewish literature. A popular midrashic story uses the same Hebrew term to describe the furnace into which Nimrod casts the boy Abraham, who has refused to acknowledge him as the sole master of the universe. Abraham, of course, emerges unscathed. When his idiot brother Haran, who doesn't believe in the real God, decides, "If Abraham can do it, so can I," he ends up like a marshmallow that has fallen into the campfire.

A more strictly canonical version of the same story is found in the book of Daniel, where Shadrach, Meshach, and Abednego (who are known as Hananiah, Mishael, and Azariah in Hebrew) refuse to worship King Nebuchadnezzar's giant idol and are thrown into a fiery furnace—in Aramaic this time, instead of Hebrew—from which all three emerge unharmed (Dan. 3).

One of the things that the Talmud is saying in invoking this image is that you *won't* be thrown into a fiery furnace for whitening your fellow's face in public. For Abraham and the three Hebrews, truth is more sacred than life itself; they wound up in a fiery furnace for refusing to affirm a lie so huge and so corrupting that they would rather die than pay it the most cursory lip service. But people who shame their fellows in public don't care *what* comes out of their mouths, as long as it serves their purposes. For them, the real difference is not between truth and falsehood; it's between effective and ineffective. If a lie will do as well as the truth, there's no need to put any premium on the latter; if the best way to get myself a promotion is to blame my mistakes on somebody else—that's *their* problem. I'm busy spending my bonus.

The indifference to truth and falsehood, the corruption of meaning that goes along with any attempt to whiten someone's face in public, will keep you *out* of the fiery furnace forever. Once you replace God or The Good or The-Divine-That-Lives-Within-

Us-All with Nimrod or Nebuchadnezzar or an all-expenses-paid trip for two, there is no need for you to be roasted alive; your sense of principle is already toast. The Talmud is trying to tell us that it is better to burn for truth and decency than rot by bearing public witness to the questionable conviction that someone who has the chutzpah to disagree with you is a cock-sucking, ass-jumping, booger-eating pedophile who gets himself off with a dildo cast from Saddam Hussein's little willy.

The idea of the fiery furnace explains the apparently irrational conduct of Chiya bar Ashi that we saw near the end of chapter 2. Having shamed his wife, as he thinks, by hiring a prostitute after abstaining from marital sex for years, he attempts to fulfill this injunction literally by jumping into the oven at home; only then does he find out that the prostitute was really his wife, who had disguised herself just as Tamar did. This didn't make him feel any better.

Jonah Gerondi, a thirteenth-century rabbi whose *Gates of Penance* still serves as a guide for Orthodox Jews interested in moral improvement, provides a slightly different perspective. Gerondi's preoccupation with penance is sometimes attributed to a crise de conscience occasioned by his having encouraged Church authorities to burn Maimonides' *Guide for the Perplexed*, an act that eventually led to the public burning of the Talmud. Rabbi Jonah eventually recanted his denunciation and did penance for it; as someone who was well known for having committed the sin that he describes here, Gerondi writes with unusual passion:

Behold a touch of murder—whitening the face of another.

His face turns white and the redness flees and it resembles

murder, and so say our rabbis of blessed memory. Secondly, the anguish of this whitening is more bitter than death, and therefore our rabbis say that a person should throw himself into a fiery furnace rather than whiten the face of his fellow in public. They do not say this about other grave transgressions and they thus compare a touch of murder with murder itself, as they say (*Sanhedrin* 74a), "Let him be killed rather than commit murder."

(SHAAREY TESHUVA 3:138)

The phrase translated here as "a touch of murder" comes out literally as "dust of murder," or better, "powder of murder." It's as much a form of murder as every astronaut's favorite drink is a form of orange juice; just add water—or in this case, blood, the blood that has fled from the victim's face—and there you have it, just about as good as the real thing:

He who whitens the face of another does not recognize the enormity of his sin. His spirit is not embittered by his transgression as that of the murderer is, and thus he is far from repentance.

(SHAAREY TESHUVA 3:140)

According to the most reliable accounts, it took Gerondi himself nine years to repent for his treatment of Maimonides, who had been dead for three or four decades by then and was as unable to enjoy his vindication as he had been to defend himself earlier.

IV

THE EMPHASIS PLACED on this prohibition against shaming another in public seems to reflect the importance of rapid-fire, take-no-prisoners debate—the sort of thing monumentalized in the Talmud—in Jewish life. Opening your mouth and letting a bullet fly out, embarrassing someone else in the course of a conversation, has become what might be called the default sin of Jewish social life, the one that people are most likely to commit before even realizing that they've done so. As long ago as 1873, a rabbi named Yisroel Meyer Kagan published a book called *Chofets Chayim* (*Who Desires Life*), about how to avoid what is called *loshn ho-ro*, "evil tongue": slander, gossip, calumny, and the like.

The book, which became so popular that Kagan is still better known by its title than by his own name—he himself is almost never called anything but the Chofets Chayim—takes its title from the Psalms: "Who is the *mentsh* who desires life, who loves days in which he sees good? Keep your tongue from evil and your lips from speaking deceitfully" (Ps. 34:13–14).

Important and influential as Kagan's book has proven, his mission, so to speak, was merely to remind us of what we should have known all along. In addition to the types of prohibited speech that we looked at earlier, the Talmud goes to some length to provide prescriptions for not hurting people's feelings inadvertently. *Sanhedrin* 94a tells us: "Do not abuse an Aramean in front of a convert down to the tenth generation." The popular Yiddish version of this goes: "*Far a ger tor men ken goy nisht sheltn*, it is forbidden to curse any gentile in front of a convert." Similarly, we are told in tractate *Bovo Metsiyo* 59b, "In the presence of someone with a relative who has been hanged, do not say, 'Hang this fish up for me.'" The Yiddish for this one comes out as, "Don't mention rope in front of someone with a relative who has been hanged."

The same sensitivity also extends to poverty and suffering, and has even had some influence on how people say their prayers. When I was a kid, the verse "I was a youth and have now grown old, and I have never seen a righteous man let down nor his seed go begging bread" (Ps. 37:25) was never recited aloud, even though it forms part of the grace after eating that is often sung at Orthodox or traditional gatherings that involve a meal. When a group came to this line, they would all drop their voices, recite the words in an undertone, and then come back singing for the closing verse of the blessing.

There were too many people sitting in synagogues in the fifties and sixties who had been let down in a big way during World War II for anyone to want to imply, even if only by inadvertent contrast, that they must somehow have deserved what happened to them, that maybe they and their murdered friends and families hadn't been righteous enough.

Similar concern was also demonstrated nonverbally. One of the funds mentioned in last chapter's list of communal agencies and relief committees was *moës khitin*, "wheat money," which started out as a way of providing poor people with flour with which to make matzohs for Passover and has evolved into a charitable fund that outfits those who can't afford it with food and other necessities for the holiday. Deliveries used to be made in middle of the night in order not to shame the recipients. I've even heard of cases in which non-Jews from other parts of town (generally employees of one of the guys on the committee) would be hired to do the driving; the names on the delivery lists meant nothing to them. No one would see the bags of groceries being dropped off on the recipients' porches or in the halls of their apartment buildings; no one not on the committee would know who wasn't making a living that year, which meant that no one could be tempted to tell someone else.

Perhaps the most dangerous kind of *loshn ho-ro* is what might be called "false truth" or "pseudo-truth": statements that are factually accurate but have been made in order to hurt someone rather than convey information or advance the cause of learning. Speech of this type is the particular preserve of the kind of *shmuck* who likes to glory in her "plain-spoken honesty," the tell-it-like-it-is, I-call-it-the-way-I-see-it sort of dork who never has a good word for anything and generally hides behind the excuse of "Well, it's true, isn't it?"

This commitment to acting like an eleven-year-old who has just looked *hypocrisy* up in a dictionary is dealt with in the Talmud in connection with weddings: What do you do when the bride is a pooch? Praising and entertaining the bride is a huge mitzvah; wedding guests still dance in front of the bride, and they used to sing her praises as they did so, a relatively uncomplicated thing until you found yourself dancing for a bride who looked like Popeye:

How do you dance before the bride? The school of Shammai says, "Describe the bride as she is." The school of Hillel says, "[Say] 'Beautiful and charming bride.'" The school of Shammai says, "And if she's lame or blind, you say, 'Beautiful, charming bride,' when the Torah commands,

'Keep far away from falsehood' "(Exod. 23:7)? The school
of Hillel said, "According to you, then, if someone makes
a bad purchase in the market, should you praise it to him
or deplore it? You've got to say, 'Praise it.'" On this basis,
the sages have said that a person should always conduct
himself pleasantly to others.

(KESUBOS 16B–17A)

In short, it doesn't cost any more to be nice than it does to
be mean, but it leaves everybody feeling a whole lot better. The
Tosfos, twelfth- and thirteenth-century commentators on the
Talmud, get to the heart of what being pleasant to others really
means:

> *The bride as she is.* [The school of Shammai says,] "If she
> has a defect, don't mention it and don't praise her, or else
> praise something about her that's nice, such as her eyes or
> her hands, if they are pretty." The school of Hillel says,
> "They should praise everything about her, for by listing
> [only] her good qualities, they imply that everything else is
> undeserving of praise."

A "truth" that is told solely for the sake of causing harm, of
putting someone in their place, or casting them in a bad light is
nothing but a stick in the hands of a bully. As anyone who has
spent more than ninety seconds in a schoolyard knows, a stick
made of wood doesn't inflict lasting damage unless you poke
someone's eye out; an unflattering "truth" can stick to a person
forever. That's why we're told that "a *mentsh* should always

be among the persecuted rather than the persecutors" (*Bovo Kamo* 93a). This doesn't mean that you're supposed to go out of your way to be victimized, but that you should aid and identify with those who are being ill-treated, rather than with those who are mistreating them.

An extreme illustration of the lengths to which you're supposed to go in order to keep someone else from being shamed is found not in the Talmud or Midrash, not in a commentary or Hasidic story, but in a Danny Dill–Marijohn Wilkin classic first recorded by Lefty Frizzell. The narrator of "Long Black Veil" has been accused of murder. The killer who fled from the scene bore a marked resemblance to him, and the judge wants to know if he has an alibi. But "I spoke not a word, though it meant my life / For I had been in the arms of my best friend's wife." The narrator hangs for murder.

Think what you want about the narrator and his best friend's wife, who might well deserve all the suffering that comes upon them; the narrator had enough concern for his best friend to spare him a lifetime of undeserved pain by letting himself be executed for a crime that he didn't commit, rather than let his friend find out that his best pal *and* his best gal had both betrayed him. The fact that sparing his friend's feelings also means protecting the reputation of his friend's unfaithful wife is just icing on this moral cake, and the narrator's inadvertent confirmation of the Talmudic statement concerning the relative gravity of both adultery and public humiliation is an unwitting interfaith bonus. The narrator, himself a persecutor, finally casts his lot with the persecuted.

In the rabbis' failure to do likewise we begin to see the source of Bar Kamtso's anger. Forgoing your own honor, suffering insults lightly, is undoubtedly a noble quality. The Mishna tells us not to be quick to anger, but the Talmud tells us:

> Those who are insulted but do not insult, who hear them-selves shamed but do not respond; who act out of love and stay happy while suffering, of them Scripture says (Judges 5:31), "Those who love Him [God] are like the sun going forth in its strength."
>
> (SHABBOS 88B)

Rashi interprets "insulted but do not insult" as meaning that "others come to them in chutzpah, not they to others." Not insulting is not always synonymous with sitting quietly. It is entirely laudable, even saintly, to decide that *you* will bear any insult. However, when you see one person insulting another and you are in a position to do something about it, you are obliged to stop it, even if you yourself would have put up with the same treatment. And that is what the rabbis did not do for Bar Kamtso. They sat and watched and refrained from what both the host and Bar Kamtso were far too ready to do. They did not get angry. They did not reprimand anybody; they sat and watched and went on with the party. And they soon paid the price for their negligence:

> Whoever can forbid the members of his household [from committing a sin] and does not do so, is punished for their sin; if it is a question of the inhabitants of his city, he is punished for *their* sin; if it's a matter of the entire world, he is punished for the whole world's sin.
>
> (SHABBOS 54B)

The rabbis attending the party could have forestalled the host's sin but did not; they failed to upbraid him, fell short of their biblically mandated obligations as Jewish private citizens and of their duties as the legislators and preceptors—the governing elite—of the Jewish people. We already know the consequences; let's see how a *mentsh* could have avoided them.

~~~~~~

FOUR

What a *Mentsh* Does

I

THE RABBIS WHO failed to reprimand their host for his treat-ment of Bar Kamtso transgressed yet another of the fundamen-tal principles of the ethical and legal system they were supposed to represent. This one had been formulated a century or so before the destruction of the Temple by Hillel the Elder, who was among the most influential and certainly the most popular of all the rabbis mentioned in the Talmud: "In a place where there are no *anoshim*, try to be an *ish*" (*Ovos* 2:5). *Anoshim* is the plural of *ish*, and as we saw in chapter 2, *ish* is one of those Hebrew words for "human being" or "person" or "man" that comes out as *mentsh* in Yiddish.

It's an unusual injunction. Rather than tell us that we should be *mentshn* and be done with it, Hillel demands that we *try* to be *mentshn*. This is not the usual way of religious or moral instruction. Imagine the Ten Commandments in a similar style: "Thou shalt try not to murder; thou shalt try not to commit adultery; thou shalt try not to steal." That one word, "try," would make guilt a thing of the past, depriving the commandments of any useful purpose. "God, I tried! How I tried!" would point to exoneration instead of frustration, and the exoneration would have to be universal. If we are to understand Hillel's statement, we need to see it in its original context:

> He used to say: A *bor* is not afraid of sin and an ignoramus cannot be pious. An overly timid person cannot learn and an irascible one cannot teach—and not everyone who does a lot of business gets smart. And in a place where there are no *mentshn*, try to be a *mentsh*.
>
> (OVOS 2:5)

The Mishna opens with two descriptions of how contrary extremes of behavior lead to the same bad ends. In the first case, we are told that the *bor* has no fear of sin and the ignoramus lacks piety, that is, is not punctilious in ritual or ethical observance. The Hebrew word *bor* has no precise equivalent in English. Maimonides defines it as a person who is "wanting in both intellect and character, that is, lacking both wisdom and morals" (Commentary on *Ovos* 2:5). A *bor* isn't afraid to sin; he is too crude, too socially and intellectually uncouth for the idea of transgression to have much meaning for him. Instead of right and wrong, he sees the world in terms of want-this, not-want-that. He does what he wants to because that's what he wants to do, and lets nothing theoretical get in his way.

The ignoramus—*am ha'aretz* in Hebrew (Yiddish: *amorets*, with the accent on the *or*)—is literally "the people of the land," a way of describing what we would call "the folks on Main Street," "the great unwashed," "plain people," "the salt of the earth," or, to put it into Aramaic, "*Kamtso bar Kamtso*— Nameless McNobody." Just plain Bill and Jane. Good, decent folk who only know what they read in the paper. In strictly Jewish terms, an *amorets* doesn't know enough to be able to understand the details of the commandments and is therefore unlikely to perform them properly, no matter how sincere or well intentioned she might be.

With respect to knowledge, let's not forget that the newspaper or Web site or blog that is the *amorets*'s chief source of information is sometimes edited by the rabbis who ignored Bar Kamtso at the party, sometimes by Mother Teresa or the Dalai Lama, and sometimes by a grand wizard of the Ku Klux Klan. The heart of the *amorets* is in the right place, but without a reasonable store of general knowledge and a mind trained to interpret and use this knowledge, she can easily go off in the wrong direction without realizing that she has done so: once again, think of well-meaning southern whites a generation or two ago who had no use for the KKK but never really questioned the morality of segregation, either.

The next pair of opposites is a little more straightforward. The overly timid student is too shy to speak up, too scared to ask questions if there's something that he doesn't understand, while a bad-tempered teacher makes all of her students overly timid: they're so afraid of an outburst of temper that they sit and nod and pretend to understand, rather than risk being yelled at or embarrassed.

Hillel's descriptions point to the social and religious consequences of these different types of unproductive behavior.

The *bor* and the *amorets* both make moral or ethical behavior into a matter of accident rather than choice. While it's possible for both to act ethically, it is difficult—if not impossible—for either to do so for ethical reasons. Since the *bor* does whatever he wants, he doesn't care if his actions are sinful or virtuous; the *amorets* doesn't always know, and doesn't even know that she doesn't know.

The *bor*, for instance, has twelve beers in an hour, starts his car, and drives off in search of a toilet. The *amorets* knows that driving after drinking twelve beers is very dangerous; she therefore has only six in the same hour, gets into the car feeling well in control of herself, and starts to drive. If she'd known about the .08 percent law, she would have obeyed it, but she's so ignorant that she's never heard of it. She understands the principle of not driving while impaired, but doesn't understand enough to know when, precisely, impairment begins. Both the *bor* and the *amorets* are driving while drunk, but they're doing it for different reasons: the *bor* doesn't care, the *amorets* doesn't know.

Likewise, those who succumb to fear of questioning and those who instill that fear both help to diminish learning and wisdom, thus preparing the ground for future crops of *bors* and ignoramuses. They sow seeds of noncultivation. Hillel's description of them is followed by a codicil that should be the motto of every MBA program on earth: "Not everyone who does a lot of business gets smart." Thinking only of business won't give you any purchase on brains. You can breeze through the financial pages and still be an *amorets*. Not everything is a matter of business, and approaching every aspect of life as a question of profit or loss will make you stupid in nonmoney matters; overriding concern for your own advantage brings only the narrowest of benefits.

After all these categorical statements, Hillel makes an abrupt change in sentence structure and issues a command: "In a place where there are no *anoshim*, you should strive to be an *ish* yourself." In a place where everybody is like the people just described, it's up to you to be the exception. You must be the *ish*.

We've already noted that *ish* can mean "person in charge, person who exercises control," and the passage that we're looking at here is a perfect example of the way in which it can be used to mean both "control over others" and "control over himself." While the *bor* is generally considered the human equivalent of a vacant lot—the major commentators point out that the basic meaning of the word *bor* is "fallow or uncultivated field," the dry raw material of the clay golem—members of the other three categories are poised on the edge of various forms of self-defeating *shmuckery*. The *amorets*'s defective knowledge of *how* to control *what* leads to a parody of self-discipline, while the shy person's fear produces self-repression rather than self-command. By being too scared to ask the necessary questions, he effectively turns himself into an *amorets* when he has every opportunity not to be one. His irascible counterpart, who doesn't control her temper at all, condemns her terrified students to a similar state of *amorets*-ism.

An *ish*, on the other hand, is a person whose demonstrable authority over himself lends his advice and opinions a certain weight with others. This kind of *ish* can likewise be called a *mentsh* in Yiddish—a person of respect, without any of that phrase's Mafia connotations—and what Hillel is saying is,

"In a place where there are no *mentshn*"—think "elders" in the sense of "respected authorities"—"try, make an effort, put yourself out, even if you'd prefer a life of cozy retirement, to be a *mentsh*." If there isn't a Man, it's up to you to be The Man, even if you are a woman.

To go back to Bar Kamtso and the banquet, then, there is no guarantee that the rabbis would have been able to stop the host from treating Bar Kamtso so badly, but they had a moral obligation as *mentshn*, as fellow humans, but even more as community leaders, to stand up and protest, to let the host know that he was out of line. Since neither Bar Kamtso nor the host can be described as a *mentsh*, it was up to the rabbis—not necessarily all of them, but any one of them, just one—to get up and do something. None of them tried, and their crisis of *mentsh*-hood changed the course of world history.

II

THE MOST COMPREHENSIVE analysis of this dictum of Hillel's is probably that of Samuel di Uzida (sometimes transcribed as Ozida, di Ozida, Uzida, or Ucedo), a sixteenth-century rabbi whose *Midrash Shmuel* was among the most popular and widely circulated commentaries on *Ovos*, the Mishnaic tractate in which Hillel's statement is found. This might not sound like much, kind of like describing it as the best-known footnote to something so insanely obscure that it's never even come up on *Jeopardy!*—"I'll take Rabbinic Apothegms for two hundred, Alex"—but *Ovos*, often called *Avot*, "Fathers," or *Pirkei Avot*, "Chapters of Fathers" (it's a question of Ashkenazic, as distinct from Sephardic, Hebrew), is the most widely read of all the sixty-three tractates of the Mishna. Its six chapters are studied in a rotating cycle on Saturday afternoons between Passover and Rosh Hashana, and at one time most men and boys—the same people who had attended the Hebrew schools described earlier—had at least some familiarity with it, even though many of them would not have been able to construe a single page of any other part of the Talmud. Its Hebrew is generally uncomplicated, its contents ethical rather than legalistic, its style generally pithy and quotable. The Saturday-afternoon study sessions soon led to *Ovos*'s being included in prayer books, which often came with Yiddish translations for the benefit of those with little or no Hebrew. If there was any part of the Talmud that uneducated people of either sex might have been expected to know, it was *Ovos*.

Di Uzida's commentary—full of practical advice in easy Hebrew—was vastly popular in Eastern Europe. Rather than a unified work reflecting the ideas of a single author, it is a collection of observations from other sources that served as a sort of *Reader's Digest* version of commentaries on tractate *Ovos*. Di Uzida's examination of the sentence that we're looking at features a lengthy quotation from the fifteenth-century rabbi Isaac Abarbanel, who says, among other things, "In a place where there are no *anoshim*"—no mentor types—"to teach you and spur you on to do the things that you are supposed to do, you yourself must spur yourself on."

Abarbanel touches here on one of the most important qualities of a *mentsh*: self-sufficiency. A *mentsh* must not only be able to rely on his own judgment and intuition when he has no one to turn to for advice, he also has to be self-motivated in acquiring the knowledge and insight that he needs to make these decisions. He has to have the confidence to act independently, especially when those around him are behaving like *shmucks* and urging him to follow suit. If you behave with kindness and consideration only when you've got your personal value's trainer and a cheerleading squad to support you, you're doing tricks, not good.

As Abarbanel goes on to say, "In a place where you can't find wise and intelligent people to teach you, you have to teach yourself." If there's no one around to show you what to do, no one whose example you can follow, *figure it out for yourself.* You're an *ish*, a *mentsh*, and not a kid: between the knowledge that you have acquired and your experience in telling right from wrong, you should be able to work it out on your own. You've got to use the one thing you've got that separates the smart from the stupid, the wise from the foolish, the *mentsh* from the *shmuck*: your *seykhl*.

III

A YIDDISH WORD, of course, taken from the Hebrew, *seykhl* comes up frequently in Yiddish conversation. It means "sense, wit, reason, understanding, brains." These are good qualities anywhere, but in a culture in which study can be said to be a form of worship, they are a basic prerequisite for full participation. *Seykhl* occupies the place in Jewish culture that legs do in marathon running—and this is one reference to Jewish culture that doesn't have to be qualified by the adjective "traditional": intelligence continues to be the most highly admired and appreciated virtue in general Jewish society, even on the part of people who lack it themselves. Whether its heroes are Talmudic scholars and biblical commentators or university professors and other intellectuals (and note the popularity of lists of Jewish Nobel Prize winners—people whose intelligence has even been fêted by the goyim), Jewish culture puts such a premium on *seykhl* that scholars and rabbis really were the ideal of a people with no generals or kings.

The one thing that rabbis and famous scholars had in common with their admirers was the basic education discussed earlier. The scholars' more sophisticated approaches to life, religious ritual, and sacred texts were gradually absorbed by their "public" in much the same way as rock 'n' roll attitudes have penetrated offices and cubicles all over the United States: the behavior and way of thinking of a prestige group filters down to less exalted members of the community, often through written works in which elite customs and behavior are described in considerable detail. The general population then adopts such attitudes and habits as are accessible to them and commensurate with their surroundings. Once a tradition takes root, it replicates itself from one generation to the next because its adherents are all drawing from the same classic sources. Where Elvis was regarded as a tasteless joke by virtually every adult of my parents' generation, his influence on every facet of American culture has been so great that his surname has become redundant. No one born and raised on this planet would even dream that I might be referring to film critic Elvis Mitchell, for instance, or that an Elvis imitator would be someone who types review copy while sporting dreadlocks to the middle of his back. And they'd be right not to do so.

Just as every rock musician owes something to Elvis, so does every rock fan, who has never even thought of picking up a guitar but likes to project the image of a certain type of rebellion. The practitioner and the nonpractitioner have both gone to the same school, as it were. That's how it was with the Jews, but without the "as it were." In an era when most people in Europe had no schooling at all and most of the nobility was semiliterate at best, future Jewish peasants and the future aristocrats of the European Jewish mind were sitting side by side in the same one-room schools, receiving the same basic education. According to the Yiddish proverb, "*Ale yidn hobn eyn seykhl*, all Jews have the same *seykhl*, all Jews think alike," because they all share the same Talmudically based way of reasoning. The nature of the Yiddish language is such that even people with no education whatever—the school system mentioned here was overwhelmingly male, in the sense that "overwhelmingly" means 100 percent; girls' education varied wildly, depending on time and place—even girls absorbed this way of thinking simply by learning how to speak: we're back to the Latin idea of conversation as the way in which you lead your life.

Ways of thought and speech that have come directly from the schoolroom can be found in virtually every area of Yiddish. Answering a question with a question, for instance. Ask someone how they are in Yiddish, and the conversation is likely to go:

PERSON 1: *Vos makht ir* [How are you]?
PERSON 2: *Vos zol ikh makhn* [How should I be]?

Aside from being a textbook example of what comics who speak a little French like to call a joke manqué, an answer of this type lets Person 1 know that nothing much has changed with Person 2 since the last time that they spoke to each other. It is a response that is rarely used with strangers, but tells anyone who knows Person 2 reasonably well not only that things are the same, but also that the unspoken second part of the sentence—"in view of the fact that I have to put up with" whatever it is that she has to put up with—need never be uttered. The interrogative tone says it all, and you're supposed to know that. *Dai le-meyvin*, as they say in Yiddish; it means exactly the same thing as *sapienti sat* does in Latin: enough for a person with *seykhl*.

It is but a step from "How should I be?" to the type of rhetorical question immortalized, if that's the word, in the famous old joke about Trotsky's supposed confession to Stalin. A telegram arrives in Moscow. It reads: "I was wrong stop you were right stop I should apologize," and is signed simply, "Trotsky." The Great Helmsman, Comrade J. V. Stalin, is beside himself with joy: Trotsky has finally confessed his guilt. Stalin is so happy that he reads the telegram out loud. A Jew, whose identity varies from one version of the joke to the next, approaches directly and begs leave to correct the Little Father of the People. "No, Comrade. It should be read like this: *I* was wrong? *You* were right? *I* should apologize?" The Jew is shot on the spot.

This type of ironic question, the kind that does not expect—or deserve—an answer, comes straight from the Talmud, and the tone of voice in which it is always delivered is redolent of Talmudic study to any native speaker of Yiddish.

A final example, one that takes us back to the origins of the ironic resignation that is so pronounced in Yiddish, involves the same Hillel whose words we have been looking at:

> The school of Shammai and the school of Hillel disputed for two and a half years. The former said, "It would be better for human beings had they not been created," and the latter said, "It is better for human beings to have been created than not to have been created." It was finally decided: "It would have been better had human beings not been created, but since they have been created, let them examine their acts."
>
> (ERUVIN 13B)

It's the typical ironic compromise. "It would have been better if you weren't here, but since you are, you might as well feel bad about it." This is the ancestor of such punch lines as "Steaks only cost a dollar at Schwartz's, but he's run out? *Nu*, when I run out, I sell them for fifty cents." There is a kind of logic at work here that cannot be described as universal. We're looking at a culture in which anybody can, and often does, say, "Sleep faster, we need the pillows," or understand and repeat something like the following Hasidic story:

> Rabbi Leib Dimimles of Lantzut was a wealthy merchant, and very learned in the Torah. It happened that he lost his money and was reduced to poverty. Rabbi Leib paid no heed to this calamity and continued his studies. His wife inquired: "How is it possible for you not to show the least anxiety?" The Rabbi answered: "The Lord gave me a brain

which thinks rapidly. The worrying which another would
do in a year, I have done in a moment."

The difference between the cultural elite and the rest of the
people was a matter of degree rather than kind, in this respect
at least. Although a certain natural endowment might have
been needed for someone to grow up to be a rabbi, this endowment was considered to be the common property of just
about everybody—which is not the same as saying that everybody made use of it. Aside from such obvious exceptions as the
mentally handicapped, these intellectual attainments were felt
to be within the theoretical reach of everyone; prolonged study
was thought to depend more on economics and disposition
than innate ability, which was generally taken for granted—
an opinion that seems to have been borne out by the rapid
progress of the children of working-class Jewish immigrants
in the learned professions in the United States and elsewhere.
Aside from access to a university system, the decisive factor was
time to study: *Tsu a gutn kop muz men hobn a gutn okher*,
for a good head, you need a good behind. This is the Yiddish
version of Blaise Pascal's remark that all human unhappiness
stems from the inability to sit still in a room. The patience to
labor over a problem until it is solved, the self-discipline to sit
and concentrate on a book, help to train our innate *seykhl* by
sharpening the ability to infer and work things out.

"If a guest coughs, it means that he needs a spoon." This
proverb provides a nice example of the kind of *seykhl* that
mentshn use. The guest, someone passing through town who
has no place of his own to spend a Sabbath or holiday, can do
nothing with the soup that is sitting in front of him because

there's no spoon at his place. Inviting a guest home for a meal is still considered one of those mitzvahs that is its own reward (especially if you get a really interesting guest who's got some good stories to tell), and the competition to get one on a Friday night could be fierce. The guest is therefore mindful of the embarrassment that even a polite request for a spoon could cause the householder and his wife. Not wishing to whiten the face of his host by calling attention to a failing, he chooses to cough instead.

The householder, who is as well versed in this way of communicating as the guest, knows that the cough is a way of not speaking. If the guest won't talk, there must be something that he would prefer not to say. The host looks to where the guest is sitting, tries to figure out what's wrong, and finally says, "Darling, why don't we give our guest a spoon." The problem is solved with almost no words being spoken.

The premium put on intelligence could lead to near-Holmesian powers of working things out. Menachem Mendel, the Rebbe of Kotzk in Poland, once had a very beautiful *esreg*, the lemonlike citron that is used in the ritual of *Sukkes*, the Feast of Booths. People go far out of their way and often well beyond what they can comfortably afford to get themselves the most beautiful *esreg* they can find, especially since an *esreg* with any kind of flaw is not valid for ritual use; even the ugly ones are beautiful, and the beautiful, it is said, are sublime. The Kotzker was so proud of this *esreg* of his that he showed it to all his students. They praised it and agreed with the Rebbe that it really was unusually beautiful. Noticing that one of his more prominent students, Wolf Landau, was absent, the Rebbe sent the *esreg* off for his inspection. Landau, who later became the

Rebbe of Strykov, looked the *esreg* over and pronounced it flawed.

Checking the *esreg* again, the other students finally noticed a tiny flaw that they had all overlooked on their initial examination. "How did you find it?" they asked Landau. "It's almost impossible to see unless you're looking for it."

"The truth is that I still haven't found it," said Landau. "But when the Rebbe wanted to hear my opinion after everybody else had already examined it and found it perfect, I figured he wouldn't be asking unless there was something wrong. Now show me the flaw."

Landau's ability to think his way through such problems made him skeptical of many *rebbes* who claimed miraculous powers. One day he was sitting in a wagon with a bunch of Hasidim on their way from one town to another, when they passed a group of gentile children playing in a field by the side of the road. Landau stroked his beard and put an otherworldly expression on his face. "That boy," he said, pointing to one of the kids, "that boy is an orphan."

The Hasidim asked the driver to stop the wagon. A couple of them got out, went over to the children, and asked after the welfare of the boy's parents. The boy told the Jews that they were dead.

The Hasidim reported back to the passengers in the wagon, and all were amazed by Landau's ability to see into the child's soul and discern his nature. Where other *rebbes* would have sat back and allowed themselves to be praised, visualizing the way the story would look in a posthumously published volume detailing all the miracles he had wrought while on earth, Landau denied having any supernatural abilities at all. "I saw that he was wearing a grown-up's hat and I asked myself, 'Where would a child get a hat like that? From his father. And why isn't his father wearing his hat? He must have no further need for it. Why doesn't he need it? If he's sick, he'd hold on to it for when he gets better. Therefore, he must be dead. And if the boy's mother were still alive, the sight of her husband's hat falling over her son's ears would probably be too much for her to bear, so I concluded that she must be dead, too."

These stories demonstrate the kind of *seykhl* that leads to *mentsh*-hood; it is rooted in learning to understand the needs and feelings of others through a dialectical process that is the same as the one used to study the Talmud and similar texts. While the *yidisher kop*, the "Jewish head," might sometimes seem to go out of its way to complicate the simple while simplifying the complex, the judicious employment of this sort of reasoning, divorced from any *shmuckish* desire for show-offy pyrotechnics, goes a long way toward helping a *mentsh* make the right decisions, especially when the proper course of action might not be immediately obvious.

IV

PUTTING YOUR *seykhl* to good use is the basis of the next remark in Di Uzida's commentary, which also seems to originate with Isaac Abarbanel: "Indeed, if we follow the path of *seykhl*, the meaning of 'In a place where there are no *mentshn*' is: people who have not conquered [or: subdued] their evil inclination. Do not learn from them. Rather, exert yourself to be a *mentsh*. For there is no *mentsh* other than he who subdues his evil inclination."

Our *seykhl* tells us not only that self-discipline makes a *mentsh*, but that there is more to a *mentsh* than we might have thought. The remark about subduing your evil inclination is based on a statement found later in *Ovos*: "Who is mighty? He who subdues his evil inclination" (*Ovos* 4:1). The word translated here as "mighty," *gibbor*, also means "valiant, courageous person; hero." It is the epithet inevitably attached to Samson's name in Hebrew and Yiddish, and would probably have been attached to Arnold Schwarzenegger's had he made any movies in Yiddish.

The idea of heroism in this context is appealing; the notion of struggling against overpowering odds and finally vanquishing the most obstreperous aspects of your personality has something very attractive about it. The idea that being a *mentsh* is a victory over selfishness and temptation, over all the *shmucks* who are dancing around you in a ring, chanting, "One of us, one of us," is difficult to resist. It is the vindication, the triumph of the moral self-reliance that the *mentsh* has developed.

Di Uzida brings this section of his commentary to a close by departing from Abarbanel and citing "an aged sage" who told him:

> *In a place where there are no* mentshn, i.e., where there are no people other than yourself, in a hidden place where there is no one to see you or know what you are doing. Do not on that account say, "I will sin; who's going to see me, who's going to know?" Even in a place where there are no people and you are in private and all alone, you must exert yourself to be a righteous, upright, and trustworthy person.

Rather than threaten divine retribution in either this world or the next for violations of *mentshly* behavior, Di Uzida takes the more stoic (some would also add, more mature) approach: act like a *mentsh* even if nobody but you will ever know the difference. Not only is *mentsh*-hood its own reward, but a *mentsh* can almost be *defined* as a person who does the right thing even though no one is looking and there is no possibility of ever being caught. Redundant as it sounds, just being a *mentsh* is the whole point of being a *mentsh*. As long as you think about getting caught, you're still thinking like a bit of a *shmuck*.

This indifference to the possibility of getting away with something makes hash of the kind of ethics games that used to be popular at parties, the ones where you have to decide which of two hypothetical courses of action to follow. You're told that you can bring lasting peace to the world by pushing a button that will cause the death of an anonymous peasant in China. You won't know anything about the person you kill—no name, no region, no nothing. You'll push a button here and he or she will drop dead over there. No one will know that the death was anything but natural. It will be just one of however many million deaths take place there every year, and no one will know but you.

In return for this action—it's so far removed from you, motivated by considerations that have so little to do with the usual reasons for murder that it can hardly be classed as such—you will improve the lives of every man, woman, and child on earth. All you have to do is press a button and kill—or maybe only *think* that you have killed; how will you ever really know?—an anonymous peasant. If you don't do it, the next outbreak of rape and violence in the Congo, probably no more than fifteen minutes away, will be entirely your fault. What would you do?

A *mentsh* would flip you the bird and refuse. The first question that he or she would ask is the one that we saw last chapter: What makes my blood redder than the Chinese peasant's? Why can't I cause the death of an anonymous hedge fund manager instead? What would I think if somebody approached a Chinese peasant with a similar offer for killing an American peasant, and the anonymous American peasant was me? Or my son? Or my daughter? Would I be willing to take a knife and cut my child's throat, if I had a guarantee that the death of the child would redeem the world?

No way, no fucking way—that's what a *mentsh* would say. Her *seykhl* would tell her that this is a sucker question: a promise of achieving the impossible, or the nearly impossible, at no cost to anyone who isn't somebody else, has to be a con. And as we've all learned from W. C. Fields, you can't cheat an honest man. An honest man or woman knows that you don't get anything for nothing and that tiny investments cannot be guaranteed to yield massive returns. A *mentsh*, or a *mentsh* who bothered to pursue the conversation and wanted to score some points, might offer the questioner a counterproposal: "I'll press the button and take a life. No problem. The benefits far outweigh any of the drawbacks. The only thing that makes me uncomfortable is the anonymity. It's cowardly, unworthy of such a noble enterprise. I'll do it, but instead of the Chinese peasant, let me push the same button and kill you instead." A *mentsh* who had reason to believe that the offer, impossible as it might sound, might be real, would say, "Forget about the peasant. Kill *me*." And a real *mentsh* might even mean it; *mentshn* have certainly died for less.

V

A *mentsh* is wise to more than the ways of the world, though; he is also wise to himself. In taking account of *ish* in the sense of "important person, person of substance, leading citizen, The Man," Di Uzida raises the kind of emotional issues that make many moralists uncomfortable:

> In a place in which there are already prominent people and eminent scholars, there is no need for you to be cautioned to try to be an *ish* and become as wise as they are, because *jealousy and ambition will force you* to try to be an *ish*. But in a place where there is no *ish*, you might let yourself go and not try to be an *ish* because you see yourself as greater and smarter than anyone else around you. Since you are greater than anyone else in the place, it will look to you as if you've already attained such perfection as is necessary. Therefore it says, "I'm warning you to try to be an *ish* in such a place. Do not be wise in your own eyes."
>
> (PROV. 3:7; my emphasis)

A *mentsh*, remember, doesn't get rid of his evil impulses, he subdues them and puts them to work for the good. Pride, lust, anger—they all have their place. The trick is learning how to keep them there. Despite the bad press that anger gets, there are sources that speak about how to put it to good use. Jewish tradition acknowledges that anger can play a useful, and even a beneficial, role in human life, as long as it is confined to the kinds of occasions mentioned by Maimonides, who said one "should get angry only about something that is worth getting angry about, in order to keep such a thing from happening again." This is the anger of prophets, social reformers, and *shmuck*-fighters all over the world. With adjustments for scale, it should have been the anger of the rabbis at the host's treatment of Bar Kamtso.

While older Jewish sources are quick to condemn anger, they don't have too many practical ideas about how to control it. Later literature is a little more inventive. Yekhiel-Meir of Gostynin, a nineteenth-century *rebbe*, wouldn't get angry at anybody on the same day as they annoyed him. Rather, he'd tell them the next day, "You got on my nerves yesterday." The admiring tone in which this story is related suggests that no one ever slapped him for doing so.

A better Hasidic story tells how Faivel of Grojec, who went on to become a prominent Polish *rebbe*, came to his teacher, Rabbi Isaac of Warka, who was already a prominent Polish *rebbe*, and complained about his father-in-law's refusal to subsidize his studies. Rabbi Isaac said, "You have every right to be angry, Faivele. But if you're going to get angry you have to change your capote," the long black coat that Hasidim still wear. Rabbi Isaac sent out to get Faivel another suit, and as soon as Faivel put it on he said, "Nu, Faivel, get mad." Faivel stood there like a golem made of clay.

Almost as sartorial is the remark of Pinchas of Koretz, a close disciple of the Baal Shem Tov, the founder of the Hasidic movement. "Since I have tamed my anger," Pinchas once said, "I keep it in my pocket. When I need it, I take it out."

Di Uzida is doing something similar with jealousy and ambition in the passage that we're looking at. Accepting the presence of these impulses and then figuring out a way to use them in a kosher manner is typical of the rabbinic approach to human nature, which can hardly be called idealistic, and Di Uzida is in fact playing off a well-known saying that claims that jealousy and lust and ambition run the world. He is saying that it is easier to rechannel evil impulses and make them good than to conquer self-satisfaction, the *shmuckish* idea of being better than others simply because you're yourself.

Regrettably, snobbery of this type has been endemic to Jewish community life for centuries and the idea of the *mentsh* seems to have developed at least in part as a corrective to such ideas of *yikhes*—pedigree or lineage—as a guarantee of human quality. The *yakhsn*, the big shot from the prominent family, would immediately see himself as the *ish* in the situations described by Di Uzida, simply by virtue of his social position and money. Yiddish characterizes this kind of person in a proverb: "*Es shteyt im nisht on tsu redn mit zikh aleyn*, he's too good to talk to himself." The *mentshly* ideal is there to remind all of us that no matter how much we might strive, we can try but we never arrive:

"Justice, justice shall you pursue" (Deut. 16:20). In the name of the *rebbe* from Lublin, it was said that what is meant here by "justice" is that if someone is convinced that he has attained the perfection of justice and that there is nothing more for him to do in this area, Scripture gives him sound advice: Pursue justice, that is to say, keep on chasing after it and never stay in one place and say that your having always acted justly up until now is enough. Real justice consists of pursuing it always, by day and by night, without any rest or relaxation. In his own eyes, a person should be as a newborn who has yet to accomplish one single thing.

It's a typically Yiddish way of looking at the world: moral progress is based on finding fault with your own current level of attainment. Rather than kvetch about the people out there, the *mentsh* learns to kvetch about himself to himself, and then do something to try to decrease his level of dissatisfaction. A *mentsh* is never 100 percent sure of himself because a *mentsh* knows his own fallibility and is always aware of the possibility of failure. In a place where everybody has learned to like themselves just as they are, a *mentsh* keeps trying to improve himself and his relations with others.

VI

THOSE OTHERS CAN be a bit of a problem, though, and a *mentsh* is well aware of the fact that not everyone else is a *mentsh*. You can be pleasant to people without necessarily believing in them, and the path from credulous naïveté to a balanced assessment of the character and motivations of the people whom you encounter is the road that leads from childhood to maturity, from the trusting *shmuckery* of the people who begged Bernie Madoff to take their money to the nuts-and-bolts skepticism of Harry Markopolos, who sat down and did the math as long ago as 1999, and was ignored until Madoff himself 'fessed up.

The transition from genial sap to full-fledged *mentsh* is what Billy Wilder's classic film, *The Apartment*, is all about. Released in 1961, it provides a more caustic look at office life in the Kennedy era than the recent television series *Mad Men*, which almost does the impossible by managing to romanticize the whole gray-flannel-suit, three-martini-lunch way of life—everything that Elvis and the Beatles and the millions of hippies who turned into yuppies in the '80s and '90s did their best to rebel against, lifestyle-wise.

The film stars Jack Lemmon as Charles "Bud" Baxter, an accountant for Consolidated Life of New York, where, as one of 31,259 employees, he works on the nineteenth floor, section W, desk 861. Baxter, who is not married, has an apartment on West Sixty-seventh Street. For the past six months, he's been lending his key to married co-workers who need somewhere to take women who are not their wives, sometimes scheduling them railway style, one after the other, on particularly busy nights. All of these co-workers are higher up on the corporate ladder than Baxter, and they all promise to put in a good word for him with Mr. Sheldrake, the head of personnel.

They're not friends of Baxter; they aren't paying him for the use of the apartment, they don't even remember to pay him for the liquor and food that he supplies. He acts like an errand boy and they treat him like one; he's the kind of a guy who just can't say no.

It started innocently enough when one of the guys in the office had to go to a banquet in the city:

His wife was meeting him in town, and he needed some-place to change into a tuxedo—so I gave him the key and word must have gotten around—because the next thing I knew, all sorts of guys were suddenly going to banquets—and when you give the key to one guy, you can't say no to another and the whole thing got out of hand.

"Out of hand" hardly does it justice: Baxter sometimes sits outside in the rain while one of his superiors has sex in his apartment. He's angling for promotion; what he gets is contempt. He's described as "some schnook that works in the office"; his place is "some schnook's apartment," and a schnook is what Baxter really is, because a schnook is a *shmuck* in English disguise.

As we saw a while ago, the English pronunciation of *shmuck* derives from a dialect form of the Standard Yiddish *shmok*. This dialect, typical of areas that are now parts of Poland, Ukraine, and Moldova, was only one of a number of Yiddish dialects and is hardly the only one to have contributed words to English. It isn't even the only dialect from which English has taken words based on *shmok*. The standard language's *shmok* form gives us the English *schmo*, a somewhat dated term for "jerk" that could do with a revival, and the even more obsolete *shmohawk* and *shmohican*, both of which can still be heard in old Warner Bros. cartoons: "What a shmohawk"; "He's the last of the shmohicans."

Shmok would also have been pronounced *shmook* in yet a third widely spoken dialect. The vowel is close, although not quite identical, to the sound that English has in *book*, *hook*, or *cook*. There is no *schnook* in Yiddish, though; it's an English word, a euphemism that substitutes an *n* for the original *m* in *shmook* in order to keep things clean. Substituting one consonant for another in order to avoid uttering a forbidden word is already familiar to us from the treatment of God's names, and the same principle is at work with *shmook* and *schnook*.

The eleventh edition of *Merriam-Webster's Collegiate Dictionary* defines *schnook* as "a stupid or unimportant person," the kind of spineless, eager-to-please, kick-me-again-but-please-notice-me underling that Jack Lemmon portrays in this movie. He's waiting for the personnel department to pay attention to him. Aside from the apartment, the only thing that distinguishes Baxter from any of the thousands of other employees in the same building is that he is the only man who takes his hat off when he gets into the elevator.

He has a crush on Fran Kubelik, one of the elevator operators, and things start to get complicated when he finds out that she has been having an affair with Mr. Sheldrake, the married head of personnel, who has given Baxter his promotion and forced Baxter to give him a key to the apartment. Although nothing at all has happened between him and Miss Kubelik (played by Shirley MacLaine), Baxter is hurt and disappointed when he realizes that she's involved with Sheldrake (Fred MacMurray), and even more shocked when he comes home on Christmas night with a woman who has picked him up in a bar, only to find Miss Kubelik in his bed. Earlier in the evening, Sheldrake let her know that he wouldn't be leaving his wife for her, and she has taken an overdose of sleeping pills.

Baxter calls the doctor in the apartment next door. The doctor, who thinks that Baxter is a compulsive womanizer over whom Miss Kubelik has tried to kill herself, has long wondered how such a *nebbish* can have such luck with women and how anybody can maintain such a frantic pace of drinking and carousing. He sits Baxter down once they're sure that Miss Kubelik is going to be all right and gives him a good, if rather brief, talking-to:

DR. DREYFUSS: I don't know what you did to that girl in
    there—and don't tell me—but it was bound to happen,

the way you carry on. Live now, pay later. Diner's Club!
Why don't you grow up, Baxter? Be a mensch! You know
what that means?

BUD: I'm not sure.

DR. DREYFUSS: A mansch [*sic*]—a human being!

Although Baxter is not supposed to be remotely Jewish,
he seems to get it. Dr. Dreyfuss (played by Jack Kruschen) is
definitely the Yiddish-cadenced conscience of the film, and
his appeal to Baxter's latent *mentsh*-hood starts to work on
Baxter, who begins to realize what a *shmuck* he has been. In
describing her affair with Sheldrake, Miss Kubelik says, "Some
people take, some people get took—and they know they're
getting took, and there's nothing they can do about it." It's a
shmuck-eat-*shmuck* world out there, and Baxter finally stands
up to it and acts like a *mentsh*, like a person with something to
them: he takes back the key to his apartment, turns in his key
to the executive washroom, and tells Sheldrake, "Just following
doctor's orders. I've decided to become a mensch. You know
what that means? A human being."

On New Year's Eve Miss Kubelik, who was about to recon-
cile with Sheldrake (whose wife has thrown him out), finds out
that Baxter wouldn't give him the apartment for the night. She
ditches Sheldrake and goes to the apartment. Baxter confesses
his love; Miss Kubelik hands him a deck of cards and says,
"Shut up and deal."

Baxter's feelings for Miss Kubelik give him the motivation
and the courage to stop being a *shmuck* and to act like a human
being instead of a lap dog. Baxter is alone through most of the
movie; even on Christmas Eve he has nowhere to go and ends up

in a bar only because Sheldrake and Miss Kubelik are using his apartment. Otherwise, he'd have been home alone. By making someone else, someone who isn't himself, his central concern, Baxter is able to step back and see what's been happening, not only with Miss Kubelik but also with himself.

His sole concern before falling for Miss Kubelik is advancement at work and he is smart enough to realize that lending out his apartment will do things for him that hard work alone, in a room filled with hundreds of others doing exactly what he's doing, is not really going to get him anywhere very quickly. Yet the higher he gets at work, the more he comes under Sheldrake's thumb; he only gets *shmuckier*, to the point where he's facilitating the bad treatment of a woman he likes and with whom he shortly falls in love.

Yet as soon as he stops thinking about his career and tries to help Miss Kubelik, not because he wants her but only because she needs help, he stops being a *shmuck*. It's the first unselfish thing he's done in the whole movie. To spare Miss Kubelik any further shame, he lets Dreyfuss assume that he was the reason that she tried to kill herself, so that when the doctor begins to talk about being a *mentsh*, Baxter is finally in a position to understand. By the end of the movie, Baxter has gone from being the kind of personality-free team player that selfish executives dream of to being the kind of player that you'd actually want to have on your team.

VII

Finding something outside of yourself on which to focus is crucial to developing into a *mentsh*. Jewish tradition seems to have stumbled upon this secret a long time ago when it started to make study into the main nonpraying activity of the religion. Though confined mostly to males until quite recently, the democratization of study became a crucial factor in the survival of post-Temple Judaism and it remains so even today. As far back as the book of Joshua, the Lord commands, "This book of the Torah shall not depart from your mouth, and you shall meditate on it day and night" (Josh. 1:8). Eventually, study became an integral part of synagogue attendance—a daily event for most Jewish men in Eastern Europe. Aside from those bits of the Bible and rabbinic literature that have been incorporated into the liturgy itself (and often tend to be rushed through without much thought), lessons in Talmud, Midrash, legal texts, and the like would be given after the afternoon and evening services by the local rabbi or better-educated laymen, who could open the texts up for people who couldn't have got through them on their own. Societies for reciting Psalms, studying the Mishna, and so on, were common in larger centers and were often organized on occupational lines: the Shoemakers' Mishna Society, the Water-Carriers' Psalm Group, and so on.

Male social life in many places consisted of evening trips to the local synagogue for communal prayer and organized study, generally seasoned with healthy portions of local and international news and gossip and often topped off with a shot of whiskey or vodka. Groups of this type tended to be made up of people who didn't study during the day and weren't always capable of doing so without help—workers, artisans, the non-elite members of the community. Gathering in this way did more than fulfill the halachic obligation to attend communal prayer whenever possible; it also served as a shield against the scorn and contempt of the more snobbish sections of the community described above.

The "common people" in the *bes medresh*—the synagogue—were doing exactly what the big shots did, and a minyan is no respecter of persons: everybody from the age of thirteen years and a day is equal. There is no big or small, no number one or number ten; the right to lead the service has more to do with who is in mourning or marking the anniversary of a family member's death than with any particular status in the community. The daily minyan is an oasis of temporary equality, a kind of circumcised Round Table in the service of an invisible king. And if the cool kids, the Mr. Sheldrakes of the local Jewish community, didn't think it was good enough for them, the hell with them, especially after the rise of Hasidism in the eighteenth century. As A. J. Heschel has pointed out:

> [The Baal Shem Tov, the founder of Hasidism] considered practical mitzvahs in the light of a person's complete personality. Nobility of character was just as important as piety. While he certainly did not deprecate the practical mitzvahs, he felt that the most important thing consisted of what a person was in his essence.

Mendel of Kotzk, the last of the Baal Shem Tov's great successors, elaborated on this theme in a slightly more pointed manner:

> "*Derekh erets*, good manners, take precedence over studying Torah." As the introduction to a book reveals the es-

sence of the book, so do a person's manners reveal the essence of his learning.

Has he really understood it, that is, or has he only absorbed a lot of facts, learned to expatiate on all kinds of concepts that have no actual bearing on the way that he lives his life? This is the kind of question that goes well beyond the problem of how people understand the books that they read. Because the line between Jewish study and Jewish prayer is often quite fine, failure to act on the moral and ethical principles set out in more academic contexts can call the depth and even the sincerity of one's commitment to the prayer book into question. Every Orthodox Jew, for instance, recites the following before retiring to bed every night:

> Master of the Universe, I forgive everyone who has angered and annoyed me or who has sinned against me—my body, my money, my honor, or anything else pertaining to me; whether willingly or unwillingly; intentionally or unintentionally; in speech or in deed; in this incarnation or another. I forgive everybody, and may no person be punished on my account.

"I'm saying this prayer because I have probably done the same, angered or annoyed or sinned against any number of people today without even realizing that I've done so. I stand as much in need of their forgiveness as they do of mine." The Baal Shem Tov and the Kotzker Rebbe want to know how many people really mean it and how many are reciting it only because it is printed in the prayer book and they're not the sort of people to skip over *anything* in the book: what's in the book ends up in their mouths, whether they're really listening to themselves or not.

The disconnect between a compulsion to say the words while paying little, if any, attention to what they mean has been around for quite a while. One of the problems that has vexed Judaism for at least two millennia already is the ease with which you can turn into a Zechariah ben Avkilos, someone who is so busy observing the rules that he forgets to look at their real purpose and thus forgets to observe himself.

In order to combat any tendencies to this type of behavior, early Hasidism counseled action:

> There is a line in the Psalms: "Turn away from evil and do good" (Ps. 34:15 [in the Hebrew]). The Hasidic interpretation of this verse is, "First do good and then turn away from evil. By doing good, you estrange yourself from evil."

Zechariah and the rabbis at the banquet with Bar Kamtso were quite good at turning away from evil; they seem to have had more trouble with the part about doing good. By fulfilling only half of the injunction, they effectively ignore evil and pay no attention to wrongs that do not seem to be of any direct concern to them.

They don't seem to notice that their failure to act degrades whatever learning they have and turns their positions into hollow mockeries of the real thing. Each becomes what Yiddish has labeled *a tsaddik in pelts*, a holy man in a fur coat, that is, a pious fraud, a little tin god, someone whose piety is a matter of outer appearance rather than inner reality. The idiom, still quite common, has been given a popular interpretation that is usually attributed to Mendel of Kotzk: a real *tsaddik*, a real holy man—*tsaddik* can also mean a *rebbe*, a Hasidic leader—warms the hearts and minds of the people around him; the *tsaddik in pelts*, the fraud in the fur, traipses about in a beautiful coat that keeps nobody warm but himself.

There are thus no *mentshn* at the banquet, nothing but *shmek* of various sizes. This lack of *mentshn* points to an apparent contradiction in Hillel's statement that none of the commentators seems to have mentioned: if you're in a place where there aren't any *mentshn*, then you're not a *mentsh*, either. Hillel is thus talking to all of *us* the way Dr. Dreyfuss talks to Baxter in *The Apartment*. Right now you might still be a *shmuck*, but if you put your mind to it, use the brain you were born with, you can change yourself very quickly. Once you start to act like a *mentsh*, you'll turn away from thinking and acting like a *shmuck*.

You need only three things that we all learned about in *The Wizard of Oz*: a brain, a heart, and some guts. You don't need separate rules for every contingency that might arise, you need one rule that's flexible enough to deal satisfactorily with *any* contingency that might arise.

FIVE

How to Do It Like a *Mentsh*

I

THE BEST SHORT example of the state of being that we're trying to avoid, the most outstanding instance of overt, utterly unself-conscious *shmuckery* that I've heard in a long time came to me by way of the Austin, Texas–based tuba and bass player Mark Rubin. Reminiscing about his first tour with a real southern bluegrass band made up of real southern white gentiles, Rubin—a native of Stillwater, Oklahoma, where his father, however, was director of the university Jewish students' center—recalled a conversation that the guys in the band held for his benefit. It concerned the morality of getting a little action on the road when there was somebody waiting for you back home. The question was: where does innocent fun stop and real cheating begin? Each member of the band had his own opinion, starting with hand-holding.

"Kissin'," said one, "just plain old kissin'."

"Bare titty," said another.

It was a six-man group and they'd gone into graphic technical detail before the last member finally weighed in. "As far as I'm concerned," Rubin swears that he said, "it isn't cheating unless you get caught."

Nobody since the dawn of time—and I'm including Moses, Jesus, Confucius, Buddha, and Dr. Phil in this reckoning—has ever been able to stop more than a small part of humanity from thinking this way. The best that anybody can do is to stop themselves and, if they're lucky, influence the people around them, especially their children, to do likewise. We need a formula or a system, something transferable that doesn't depend upon a particular person's character or good nature. We're looking for something that anybody can do, that doesn't require too much theoretical knowledge or impose too much of an intellectual burden; something that can be used by everybody and taught to anybody, regardless of who they are, where they live, or what they believe, and can give any of them the power to be a *mentsh* in a place where there are no other *mentshn*. We're looking for a way to conduct ourselves that has the potential to make a statement like the following obsolete: "Pray for the welfare of the state. If not for fear of it, we'd have swallowed each other alive" (*Ovos* 3:2).

While this might look like the usual vulgar, law-and-order Hobbesianism that pops up on television commercials during campaigns for get-tough governors and crime-smashing DAs, it's considerably more complex than that and touches on a theme that hasn't yet been mentioned but cannot really be ignored any longer: the idea that too many *shmucks* can wreak havoc on democracy and that loss of *mentsh*-hood makes self-government a joke.

The Mishnaic statement above is attributed to Rabbi Chanina, the Deputy of the Priests, who lived at the same time as Zechariah ben Avkilos and Rabbi Yochanan, whom we saw asking for the town of Yavne at the end of chapter 2. Like them, he saw the Temple destroyed; unlike either of them, Chanina was a Temple official and the Temple was where he spent most of his time. Although his title, "Deputy of the Priests," makes him sound rather like the Barney Fife of animal sacrifice (older readers might prefer to imagine Chester, as played by Dennis Weaver, on *Gunsmoke*: "Bullock's ready, Mr. High Priest"), Chanina's job was closer to that of vice president or first runner-up; he had to be ready to stand in for the High Priest, should the latter prove unable to perform his duties for any reason.

Chanina lived at a time when relations between Rome and Judea were approaching their nadir, and the savagery with which the Romans put down the revolt that lasted from 66 to 73 C.E. aroused negative comment in Rome itself. Meanwhile, the Jews seem to have been as busy fighting each other as they were with struggling against the Romans, with the happy result that there were at least two separate wars going on much of the time, one against the Romans and one against ourselves.

In the midst of all this, Chanina was an outspoken peace-nik. In *Sifre*, a collection of midrashic commentaries on the books of Numbers and Deuteronomy, he is quoted as saying, "Peace is great, for it outweighs the whole work of creation" (*Sifre, Naso*, 42). In the remark quoted in *Ovos*—again, considered so worthy of preservation that it was included in the *Harry Potter* of rabbinic literature, the one work that people who don't read rabbinic literature read, enjoy, and reread—his mention of "the state" must have caused the jaw of anybody who heard him say it to drop. Chanina is talking about Rome here, and instead of saying "the state" might just as well be saying "the enemy," or even "the empire," with all of that term's *Star Wars* implications.

Although we don't know whether he made this statement before or after the destruction of the Temple, his comment on the nature of Jewish society at the time strikes a realistic, if not terribly hopeful note. "Swallow each other alive" implies that internecine troubles arise simply because they can; no excuse is necessary because an excuse can always be found. As long as people behave like cannibalistic children, they're going to need to have a teacher in the room at all times, and if subjection to a foreign power is what it takes to make them behave—it's bad, but it beats the alternative.

If Cain can kill Abel in a dispute over the location of a Temple that was nowhere near to being built when the population of the world numbered only four, just imagine how their descendants will act when they're able to assemble armies. Chanina was saying what everybody at the time already knew: if we weren't going to submit to Rome, we'd have to submit to whatever gang of criminals or ideologues was in power *this* week, wreaking vengeance on people for living in the wrong part of town, going to the wrong synagogue, or having different ideas of how to prepare for apocalypse. The guys who burned the food supplies were determining foreign policy. Imagine Jim Morrison in command of the Continental Army instead of George Washington: when "No one here gets out alive" is a re-cruiting slogan, you can't place much faith in a lasting victory.

When a guy like Chanina, for whom peace ranks on a level with bringing the world into being, says that the thousands of Jews killed by the Romans during the revolt in Judea were a drop in the bucket compared to the numbers who would have been killed if they had had free rein to kill each other, you can probably take his word for it. Whatever the historical status of the story of Bar Kamtso and the banquet, Chanina's contemporaneous remark confirms its picture of Judean society, especially the Judean elite at the time, and has plenty to say to us today.

If we're all such *shmucks* that we're better off as the subjects of despotic conquerors than as free members of an independent commonwealth—for the simple reason that our *shmuckery* makes community in any meaningful sense of the term impossible—then we're doing something very wrong. The tragedy here is that there really was a remedy immediately at hand, in the hands, indeed, of the rabbis at the banquet, but everybody was so busy trying to get what he felt was coming to him—power, vindication, his own way—that the welfare of everybody else was quickly forgotten. No matter how dire the situation, the competing factions continued to commit the cardinal Jewish social sin, the one that marriage and procreation are supposed to make impractical, if not impossible: they kept on putting themselves and their own narrow—you could even say sectarian—desires ahead of the general welfare.

II

IF EVERYBODY INSISTS on being the cantor, there is no hope of a minyan: as long as having your way is the most important thing in the world to you, you can't really help but feel resentful and envious of anyone who gets their way when you do not. Unless they hold public office and you're able to wait four years and hope you can be elected to replace them, there usually isn't much you can do about it except sit and stew and plot their demise.

In that sense, envy can be described as the egotistical sin par excellence, the most thoroughly selfish of all, because its sole meaning, its only goal, consists in harming someone else. Aristotle defined it as "pain at another's good fortune," and where most other sins—pride, avarice, lust, even anger—involve getting or taking something for oneself, the essence of envy lies in depriving someone else.

The obsession with the evil eye in so many otherwise disparate cultures bears witness to a deep appreciation of the all-too-central place of envy in so many human characters. Children, babies even, will cry and even hit to get something that they want only because someone else—often someone of similar or smaller size—has it. Perhaps it's a legacy of Cain and Abel fighting over the location of the Temple, but the pleasure of depriving others of something is often far greater, and far more motivating, than whatever it is that they're being deprived of. Just look at *shmucks* who cut others off and insist on nosing their way from lane to lane in traffic that isn't moving at more than five miles per hour. They know that they're not going to arrive any faster, they just can't live with the idea of having someone come before them.

The Talmud takes up the near universality of envy in a very brief and slightly cryptic passage:

What should a person do in order to live? Put himself to
death. What should he do to die? Bring himself to life.

(TOMID 32A)

Rashi explains the real meaning of these answers:

Put . . . to death: Let him bring himself low. *Bring . . . to
life*: Let him raise himself up. Doing so will cause people
to cast an evil eye on him; they will envy him and he will
die. Our sages have taught that a person who wishes to live
should lower himself so that people will take pity on him
and he will live for many years. Let him keep himself from
pride lest his days grow short and he die before his time.

To hear Rashi tell it, in this passage at least, morals have
nothing to do with it; humility and all the virtues associated
with it are really about self-preservation. The fall that goeth
after pride is the result of a swift kick from behind by a steel-
booted evil eye.

That's not what Rashi really means, of course; he's speaking from the same strictly practical point of view as the Talmud
in this passage. Nonetheless, we can see the importance of
the evil eye here and the idea that there is almost no limit to
human invidiousness. There's a proverb in Yiddish—"*Boday
zikh eyn oyg, abi yenem tsvey*, I'd gladly lose one eye, as long
as the other guy loses two"—that says it all. And not just in
Yiddish. The image goes back at least as far as Aesop and can
be found in such unexpected places as John Gower's almost
endless fourteenth-century English poem, *Confessio Amantis*,

and Robert Burton's *Anatomy of Melancholy*. Joseph Jacobs's rendering of Aesop gives the whole story in the form probably most familiar to readers of English:

> Two neighbours came before Jupiter and prayed him to grant their hearts' desire. Now the one was full of avarice, and the other eaten up with envy. So to punish them both, Jupiter granted that each might have whatever he wished for himself, but only on condition that his neighbour had twice as much. The Avaricious man prayed to have a room full of gold. No sooner said than done; but all his joy was turned to grief when he found that his neighbour had two rooms full of the precious metal. Then came the turn of the Envious man, who could not bear to think that his neighbour had any joy at all. So he prayed that he might have one of his own eyes put out, by which means his companion would become totally blind.
>
> Vices are their own punishment.

The moral, such as it is, is the same on every occasion. Apart from the fact that there are plenty of *shmucks* out there who think and act in precisely this fashion and are happy to punish themselves, as long as they think that you've been punished more (many of them would deny doing so, and would actually believe their own denials), we've already seen that Jewish tradition would rather retrain such urges, send them to school, as it were, than try vainly to put them to death. As we are told in another Talmudic statement: "A man envies everybody except for his child and his student" (*Sanhedrin* 105b). Rather than waste our time trying to stamp out a fire that's just going to reignite, we're better off to take it and use it for something of some immediate benefit to somebody, if not ourselves then somebody else.

Well before the Talmud, the Bible recognized this problem and prescribed a way to treat the property of your enemy:

> If the ox or donkey of your enemy has gone astray and you encounter it, return it to him. If you see your enemy's donkey lying down beneath its load and would like to refrain from lifting it up, lift it up anyway.
>
> (EXOD. 23:4–5)

Note that the idea of having an enemy is taken for granted. The context of the commandment makes it clear that the Bible isn't talking about ex-Nazis or members of the Aryan Nations here; by enemy, it means a member of the same community as you, the kind of person who is called "fellow," "brother," or "sister" in more positive exhortations to benevolence, the kind of enemies who are so hard to distinguish from friends that they can end up with the friends' invitations by mistake. We're dealing with malevolence of feeling on either end here—unexplained and possibly inexplicable—and the biblical approach foreshadows the rabbinic realism that develops later.

Jewish ethics know a lot of things, but the thing that they know best is the Jews. Let's not forget that many of the rabbis mentioned in this book, along with many more whose names have not come up, did not earn their living as rabbis, especially those who lived in ancient times. Hillel started out as a woodcutter; Rashi is said to have owned vineyards and made wine; Isaac Abarbanel was treasurer to King Alfonso of Portugal;

many of the Hasidic *rebbes* mentioned had businesses of one sort or another, at least until they became established as *rebbes* (and often even afterward); and the Chofets Chayim ran a store for a time.

These rabbis formulated their ethical ideas on the basis of personal observation and experience, and many of them had plenty of experience on which to draw. They had both personal and business dealings with the descendants of the people who kvetched their way through the Exodus, and they thus had no difficulty in accepting the idea that there are probably a lot of people out there that you don't like and who aren't really wild about you, either. These rabbis had seen enough to know that no command, no legislation, no promise of eternal bliss or threat of endless punishment was going to change what, reluctantly or not, they had to admit to be human nature. If Eve could be afraid that Adam might start playing footsy with a rival who didn't exist; if Cain could kill Abel over a piece of real estate that wasn't going to be developed for another couple of millennia—if there were three different enemies when there were only four people in the world, for God's sake, there doesn't seem to be much hope of changing the basic character of humanity. All we can do is decide where to place the emphasis.

Enemies, then, are a given. We're going to dislike and be disliked, and the Jewish people have distinguished themselves on both sides of that "and." The one thing that we understand, until it's time to start dealing with other Jews about Jewish communal politics, is that nobody has ever really benefited from refusing to adopt a live-and-let-live attitude to "enemies," people and groups whom you might not like, but who have no intention of acting on their personal enmity or of marching toward your house in a uniform that bodes you no good. Just because someone is your enemy is no reason to hate him. The book of Leviticus commands us to love our neighbor, and we have to pause to figure out what that means; in the book of Exodus, which comes before Leviticus, we receive a much more definite command: Do not be a *shmuck* to your enemy.

And let's not forget the donkey. *He's* the one doing the real suffering, and it is your responsibility to do whatever you can to help alleviate that suffering. As a donkey, he isn't responsible for the misdeeds or bad attitudes of his owner, not even if he's Francis the Talking Mule and his master, Donald O'Connor, has taken a sudden turn for the bad. Talmudic tradition places a very high value on kindness to animals, and general directions for their care crop up alongside the laws of saying the Grace After Meals or greeting a heathen during a sabbatical year:

> It is forbidden for a man to eat before he feeds his beast, as it is written (Deut. 11:15), "And I shall give grass in your fields for your cattle," and only afterward, "and you shall eat and be filled."
>
> (BROKHOS 40A; GITIN 62A)

We're told in Proverbs that a just man looks out for his animal (Prov. 12:10). Since your enemy's donkey can't look after itself, you—as somebody who can care for both yourself and the donkey—are obliged to look after it, no matter whom it belongs to. Indeed, you have a greater obligation to your enemy than to your friend: "If your friend's donkey needs unloading and your enemy's needs loading [because it has fallen], your enemy's takes precedence, in order to make sure that you rein in your evil inclination" (*Bovo Metsiyo* 32b), even though your friend's donkey is in a more painful position than your enemy's. Since your inclination in all matters would be to let your enemy and his donkey ride straight to hell together, this ruling actually overrides the Torah's teaching on the suffering of animals in order to make a point about the need for humans to get along.

This occasional tendency to place morality ahead of revelation is one of the nicest features of the Talmud. Anybody who's read the duller parts of the Pentateuch—the laws, the begats, the architectural specs for the Tabernacle—is aware that biblical religion had no problem with capital punishment. People could be put to death for all the usual crimes—murder, adultery, kidnapping, and so on—and also for some that only Jews can commit: gathering sticks on the Sabbath, unauthorized manufacture of anointing oil, consumption of leaven on Passover, and similar offenses against cultic rules. Yet the Mishna tells us:

> A Sanhedrin that kills one person every seven years is said to be callous with regard to human life. Rabbi Elazar ben Azariah said: Make that every seventy years. Rabbi Tarfon and Rabbi Akiva said: Had we been on the Sanhedrin, no one would ever have been killed.
>
> (MAKKOS 1:10)

Despite the fact that the Sanhedrin ruled on many cases for which death in one form or another was the biblically ordained punishment, we are told here that it was so loath to apply the death sentence that an execution every seven years was considered a sign of unbridled cruelty. Rabbi Akiva, who along with Rabbi Tarfon would effectively have abolished the death sentence altogether, is the single most important figure in the Talmud, and could credibly be described as its leading man. What Moses is to the Bible, Akiva is to the Talmud: the hero—a modern biography is subtitled *Scholar, Saint, and Martyr.* His importance and prestige were not even diminished by his claim that Bar Kokhva, the leader of a revolt against the Romans, was also the Messiah. Yet here he is, stating explicitly that judicial executions are always to be avoided. Although capital punishment remained on the books, it was rarely carried out. The opinions of Elazar, Tarfon, and Akiva all indicate the way in which morality can sometimes trump revelation in the world of the Talmud, the last place where people unacquainted with it might expect to find *mentsh*-hood conquering halacha.

The main point behind helping your enemy is that the animal shouldn't be made to suffer for something that has nothing to do with it. Just as important, though, is the heuristic, the educational, effort of restraining your evil impulse in a situation where the right thing to do is clear. If you should thus find yourself confronted with a less cut-and-dried dilemma, you'll know what to do and will recognize the evil impulse when it comes to you in the guise of a lawful and sometimes even laudable activity.

There's a story about how a poor widow once went to Rabbi Aaron of Karlin (died 1772), saying that her daughter had been engaged for two years already, but her fiancé was about to break off the engagement because he still hadn't received the fifty-ruble dowry that he had been promised. Rabbi Aaron, yet another great Hasidic leader (there aren't many edifying tales about the crummy ones), went over to his dresser, took out fifty rubles, and gave it to the woman.

An hour later she was back. The wedding had already been arranged, but the poor girl had no wedding gown and her mother didn't have the five rubles to get her one. Rabbi Aaron went over to his dresser, much more slowly this time, took out five rubles, and gave them to her:

A Hasid who happened to be present asked, "The fifty rubles I understand; providing for a bride is one of the biggest mitzvahs there is. But the five rubles for the dress? Wouldn't it have been a bigger mitzvah to buy ten pair of shoes for orphans?"

"I had the same idea," said Rabbi Aaron. "Better to buy ten pair of shoes for poor orphans than a silk wedding gown. But then I started to wonder where this thought was coming from—the good inclination or the evil one—and I decided that it was the evil. If it's coming from the good inclination, I thought, why was he silent about it until now, when the woman came to beg for money for the gown? Why didn't he tell me to buy shoes for the orphans yesterday? So I figured that this must be coming from the evil inclination, and I don't take advice from the evil inclination."

There are two matters to consider here. Providing for the bride without providing her a gown is only doing half the job. There's a well-known axiom to the effect that once you start on a mitzvah, you're supposed to see it through to the end, and though Aaron doesn't mention it explicitly, this is the basis on which the girl's mother has had the apparent chutzpah to come back so soon for a second donation. On a less obvious level, Aaron is self-aware enough to know that if he doesn't pay for the dress, he's not going to use the money to buy shoes for the orphans: he'll think about it, put it off, think about it some more, put it off again, and then forget all about it.

In the usual scheme of things, shoes for orphans will always outrank a fancy dress, even if it's a bridal gown. In the present context, though, the shoes are a distraction, a way of not fulfilling an obligation that you've undertaken by convincing yourself that you're wriggling out of your duty for the sake of something better; that you're cheating in a kosher way.

In Yiddish, this is called *a kosher khazer fisl*, a kosher little pig's foot, the legitimate-seeming enticement to something that really isn't kosher at all. The idea goes back to the description of the pig in the eleventh chapter of Leviticus: "And the pig, because it parts the hoof and is cloven-footed, but does not chew the cud, is unclean to you" (Lev. 11:7). If you look at it the right way, the pig can pass for kosher. A well-known Midrash talks about how the pig lies on its back, to make sure that you can see its hooves, and says, "Eat me, I'm kosher" (*Genesis Rabbo* 65:1).

The evil inclination stuck out a kosher pig's foot in the form of the orphans' shoes, but Rabbi Aaron is too smart to go for it. When *seykhl* meets emotion, it can teach even the heart to think.

III

As we can see with Rabbi Aaron, a thinking heart is a wonderful thing, but it has to have something to think about. The favorite traditional subject is controlling the evil inclination in order to develop a capacity for mercy toward people and animals alike, those we don't like just as much as those we do. Very broadly speaking, these are the two major characteristics that distinguish the *mentsh* from the *shmuck*; they're also what makes it possible for *shmucks* to change their behavior and turn themselves into *mentshn*, or for *mentshn* to fall off the wagon, so to speak, and take the long plunge into *shmuckery*. The *shmuck* isn't really evil; he's just got a heart that acts before it thinks—mostly because it rarely thinks, and when it does, tends to do the wrong kind of thinking. It can't really distinguish between what it should be doing and what it feels like doing.

According to the Midrash, "Whoever is soft when he should be hard will finish by being hard when he should be soft" (*Ecclesiastes Rabbo* 7:24). The example it gives is King Saul, who first disobeyed God's orders and spared Agag, the king of Israel's bitterest enemy, Amalek, then balanced out this misguided kindness by having eighty-five Israelite priests put to death because of a mistaken suspicion that they were in league with David to overthrow him.

Saul was mentally ill; the average *shmuck* is simply out for herself and thinks that acting like a conscienceless jerk might be the best way to do so. The problem is that amoral behavior tends to have long-term benefits only for those who really are amoral and whose consciences really won't have anything to say. As the Baal Shem Tov once described it:

A poor man asked his rich brother: "Why are you wealthy, and I am not?" The other answered: "Because I have no scruples against doing wrong." The poor brother began to misconduct himself but he remained poor. He complained of this to his elder brother, who answered: "The reason your transgressions have not made you wealthy is that you did them not from conviction that it matters not whether we do good or evil, but solely because you desired riches."

If you really want to be a *shmuck* because you think that being a *shmuck* is the way to be, no one can stop you. If, however, you turn yourself into a *shmuck* in order to get something else—money, friends, esteem—you'll simply end up as a failed *shmuck*, a wannabe whom nobody likes and who can't figure out why the other *shmucks* are getting ahead while he gets treated like a *shmuck* even by the other *shmucks*.

Once again, Hillel has the answer, in a couple of remarkable passages, both of which occur on the same page of the Talmud. Hillel was renowned for his mild disposition, remarkable patience, and willingness to go out of his way to make things easy for others, especially in his rulings on Jewish law. The first passage is a compelling demonstration of the futility of *shmuckery*, especially *shmuckery* as a cold-blooded tactic or strategy. It begins with an admonition, then gets straight to the story:

Let a person always be mild like Hillel and not irascible like Shammai. It happened once that two men made a bet: "Whoever can provoke Hillel to lose his temper will get four hundred zuzim." One of them said, "I'm going to do it."

It was a Friday and Hillel was washing his hair. The man passed by the door of Hillel's house, saying, "Is there

a Hillel here? Is there a Hillel here?" Hillel put something
on and went out to greet him.

"What is it that you want, son?" he said.

"I have a question to ask you."

"Ask away, son, ask away."

"Why do Babylonians have heads shaped like eggs?"

(SHABBOS 30B–31A)

Zuzim is the plural of zuz, which was a unit of currency,
and four hundred of them seems to have been a conventional
number that meant "a lot of money." The same sum is the subject of a dispute in a famous passage in *Ovos de Rabi Nosn*, a
later elaboration of *Ovos*, in which Rabbi Akiva fines a man for
humiliating a woman in public. The guy who is out to humili-
ate Hillel here takes care to turn up on Friday, the eve of the
Sabbath. Hillel is preparing himself for the holy day and probably has a lot of other things to do, so the guy is hoping that
he'll be a little bit on edge, slightly impatient to get rid of him
so that he, Hillel, can devote himself to his Sabbath prepara-
tions. Asking deliberately silly questions is just another strata-
gem to try to push Hillel over the edge.

The bettor isn't very bright, though. He starts off by asking,
"Is there a Hillel here?" This is rather like banging on the door
of the White House and yelling out, "Someone named Obama
live here?" Hillel was the *nassi*, the head of the Sanhedrin, and
occupied a position somewhere between president and chief
justice of the Supreme Court. He was one of the most prominent people in the country.

Hillel is also said to have come to the land of Israel from
Babylon at the age of forty, so the question about the shape of

Babylonians' heads isn't only silly, it is a deliberate provocation, again like asking Barack Obama, "Why do all Hawaiians
have such big ears?" Hillel isn't biting, though:

> Hillel said, "Son, you have asked a great question. It's be-
> cause they have no skillful midwives."
>
> He went away, waited for an hour, came back, and said,
> "Is there a Hillel here? Is there a Hillel here?"
>
> Hillel put something on and went out to meet him. He
> said, "Son, what is it that you want?"
>
> "I have a question to ask you."
>
> "Ask away, son, ask away."
>
> "Why are people from Palmyra bleary-eyed?"
>
> Hillel said, "Son, you have asked a great question. It's
> because they live in places with a lot of sand."
>
> He went away, waited for an hour, came back, and said,
> "Is there a Hillel here? Is there a Hillel here?"
>
> Hillel put something on and went out to meet him. He
> said, "Son, what is it that you want?"
>
> "I have a question to ask you."
>
> "Ask away, son, ask away."
>
> "Why do Africans have wide feet?"
>
> (SHABBOS 31A)

The third such question would reasonably send just about
anyone around the bend. These are klutz questions on a par
with "What makes the Hottentot so hot? What puts the ape in
apricot?" but without Bert Lahr to deliver them. Hillel clearly
knows that he's being baited, yet seems indifferent to being
bothered. He's as cool as they come; having put his clothes off

and on three times in as many hours, it's possible that he was the inspiration for Isaac of Warka's idea about changing your jacket before you're allowed to get angry.

The *shmendrik* keeps going, though. He wants his four hundred zuzim:

> Hillel said, "Son, you have asked a great question. It's because they live in marshy regions."
>
> He said, "I have many questions to ask, but I'm afraid to in case I anger you."
>
> Hillel put something on and sat down before him and said, "Ask all the questions you've got."
>
> "Are you the Hillel who is called the *nassi* of Israel, the head of the Sanhedrin?"
>
> "Yes."
>
> "If you are, may there not be many like you in Israel!"
>
> "Why not, son?"
>
> "Because I lost four hundred zuzim on account of you."

The guy is starting to lose his temper himself.

> Hillel said, "Take it easy. Better for you to lose four hundred zuzim and a further four hundred zuzim, than that Hillel should lose his temper."
>
> (SHABBOS 31A)

Matzoh wouldn't melt in his mouth. Hillel seems to have no trouble keeping his temper. The guy who has made the bet wants to embarrass Hillel in public—note that this all takes place out of doors, somewhere in front of Hillel's house—by having Hillel lose his temper and embarrass *him*. He thought he'd make an easy four hundred zuzim by behaving like a *shmuck*. Had he paid more attention in Hebrew school instead of fooling around, trying to figure out ways to provoke his betters, he would have realized that he wasn't going to get too far with *Ish* Number One, the leading *mentsh* in the country.

Note the subtlety of Hillel's closing put-down. Anyone who could afford to bet four hundred zuzim on anything had plenty of money to spare. What Hillel is saying is, "You can lose as much money on me as you want, rich boy, there isn't enough of it to make me betray my principles." Of course, it's unlikely that the guy who made the bet got much of this; he was too busy thinking about his four hundred zuzim. Hillel's renowned lenience in halachic decision contrasts with his apparent inflexibility about losing his temper, and he is a perfect illustration of psychologist Lawrence Kohlberg's maxim, "There are exceptions to rules . . . but no exceptions to principles."

The admonition at the beginning of this anecdote reminds us of why it is being told in the first place. We're being counseled to be like Hillel rather than his great rival and antagonist, Shammai. Hillel is described as "mild." The Hebrew could also be translated as "modest, humble," or even "meek" and is the adjectival form of the noun that is used to characterize Zechariah ben Avkilos in the story of why Jerusalem was destroyed. Hillel's mildness or humility is the real thing. Even though he's head of the Sanhedrin, he doesn't live in a palace, doesn't seem to have any servants, and isn't too grand to come outside in his robe to answer questions that he already knows are going to be stupid. When the same word is used about Zechariah, it's a bitter circumlocution, a disaffected way of describing the haughty pomposity that he maintains in the direst emergency.

Similarly, Shammai, who probably has the worst temper in the entire Talmud, is described as a *kapdan*, the same word that was used to characterize the person who was pronounced unfit to teach in the passage from *Ovos* discussed in chapter 4. And who said that the *kapdan*, the irascible, bad-tempered person, can't teach? Hillel, who has just successfully managed to face down a challenge to his whole philosophy of interpersonal relations.

The text then continues with a brief anecdote about a non-Jew who wants to convert to Judaism, but only on condition that he not have to learn the Oral Law, the traditions and methods of interpretation represented by the Talmud and the rabbis who are quoted in it. His going to the two most prominent teachers of the time with such a request must have been yet another provocation, rather like asking Jean-Paul Sartre for philosophy lessons while telling him to put a lid on the French. Shammai chases him away; Hillel demonstrates the absurdity of the heathen's request and wins him over.

A story about another proselyte follows:

On another occasion a heathen came to Shammai and said, "Convert me, provided you can teach me the whole of the Torah in its entirety while I stand on one foot."

Shammai pushed him away with the measuring rod that he was holding.

The heathen went to Hillel, who converted him and said, "Do not do what is hateful to you to your fellow. That

is the whole of the Torah in its entirety. The rest is commentary. Go and learn."

(SHABBOS 31A)

This is one of the best-known and most frequently cited
passages in the Talmud. It is often adduced as proof of Hillel's
wisdom and good nature, especially as contrasted with Shammai's grumpy rigidity. I've lost count of the number of times
I've seen it described as "the Golden Rule, but phrased nega-
tively" or something to that effect. None of these statements is
wrong, but there's a lot more going on here than simple antici-
pation of Jesus.

IV

To LOOK AT Hillel's statement as a mere forerunner or prelude
to Jesus's more upbeat formulation about half a century after
Hillel's death is to do an injustice to both Hillel and his idea.
Although Jesus seems to quote this passage almost word for
word in the Gospel of Matthew, we'll see that there is quite
a gap between "do unto others" and "don't do unto others,"
and that the difference is more than a matter of grammar or
rhetoric.

Negative expression comes naturally to people like Hillel
and Shammai who spend much of their time codifying prohibitions and ruling on the extent of their application, but Hillel's
formulation has more to do with the rabbinic view of human
nature, which lies at the root of many of the prohibitions, than
with the fine points of legal terminology. The ubiquity of enemies and envy suggests that putting oneself into another's

place is not always as easy and almost never as automatic as we might wish; human beings are so various, so unpredictable, that it can be dangerous to assume that everyone would necessarily like you to treat them in the same way as you'd like them to treat you. Once we have taken care of the obvious physical needs common to all members of the species—food, shelter, clothing, and so on—we often lack the insight into others that will allow us to treat them in the way that they'd like to be treated. This is especially true with respect to the way they'd like to be treated while going about their business when there is nothing particularly wrong.

Look at the commandment about the donkey in Exodus. *You* would help anybody in such a situation, even an enemy, if only out of concern for the donkey. If it were *you* who was standing beside a collapsed donkey, you'd be willing to accept help from anyone, including your bitterest enemy. What happens, then, if your enemy hates you so much that he refuses your help and tells you to go away? He'd rather watch the donkey die than feel indebted to you for anything. And now that you've offered to help, he hates you even more; now that he's turned down your offer, you hate him even more and want to get back at him for making a fool of you in public. And that's about as far as "do unto others" can take you. It's still a fairly long way, but it cannot get you inside of someone who doesn't share your values.

Hillel doesn't demand any insight into others. He already understands that our knowledge of anybody else is a hit-and-miss proposition at best, especially when it comes to those matters of the heart that are always concealed from everybody but the subject. Treating others as if they shared all of our innermost tastes and feelings and longings—as if they were us, that is—can easily turn into an exercise in egotism that is ultimately not very different from giving them orders about how to think, feel, and live—because we, of course, know better. Knowing how we'd want *our* desires to be fulfilled doesn't tell us how others would like to look after theirs. Proceeding as if we already knew what they want could be perceived as patronizing, or even offensively paternalistic.

The story of the convert is there to show why a person should always be as unassuming as Hillel; the one about the bet to make him lose his temper shows just how mild he was. The guy who made the bet is deliberately violating the "do not do unto others" rule in order to win a substantial sum of money. It's unlikely that he would want Hillel hanging around his house, yelling out his name, and asking him stupid questions, especially not when he was trying to do something that needed to be finished fairly quickly.

Hillel, who might not have guessed that the guy was acting on a bet, refuses to take the bait. Instead of yelling at the guy or dismissing his questions or even telling him to come back at another time when he wouldn't be quite so busy, he submits to the summonses and questions with grace and forbearance, answering them to the best of his ability and ignoring any personal insults. Remember, he started out as a woodcutter, near the bottom of the social scale, so poor that another Talmudic passage claims that dead people who plead poverty as an excuse for not studying are asked by the heavenly court, "And were you poorer than Hillel?" (*Yoma* 35b). During his time as a penniless *shlepper*, which is supposed to have lasted well into middle age, he must have been spoken to in just the same way as the bettor talks to him: "Is there a Hillel here?"

Hillel doesn't let it get to him, though. He won't speak that way to another person. He takes the questions at face value, answers them as well as he can, and is quite willing to sit and answer any remaining questions that the guy might have. And it's that—refusing to treat the bettor like the *shmuck* that he is because Hillel doesn't like to be treated like a *shmuck*—that finally drives the guy over the edge. He knows that he's acting like an asshole—hell, he's doing it on purpose, and it's driving him crazy that Hillel seems to be immune to it. If he can't get Hillel to behave like a *shmuck*, he'll have to give up all that money. Finally, though, *he* loses it and finishes by cursing Hillel: "May there not be many like you in Israel" is a fancy way of saying, "May you have no disciples or descendants, may you fail as a teacher and die without issue."

Anybody would have been forgiven for losing his temper over such a remark, but Hillel takes it in stride and asks the guy why he feels that way. Once he finds out, Hillel merely lets him know that he'll lose his four hundred zuzim on every subsequent attempt, because he'll never get Hillel to lose his temper.

Hillel can see that the money is a side issue; it's about control, management in contemporary terminology, specifically, the management of emotion and inclination. By telling the guy that he would only lose more money by continuing to try to anger him, Hillel is saying that now that he understands what's happening here, don't expect him to do the "benevolent" thing and lose his temper in order to help the other guy get his four hundred zuzim. Indeed, such faux benevolence would only encourage further *shmuckery* on the bettor's part.

V

HILLEL KNOWS WHAT he *doesn't* want, and will thus never deliberately do anything to cause another person to lose his temper: the pique that has no chance to happen is the one that leads to harmony. While we are often at a loss to describe our desires in any but the most general terms, there isn't anyone who's not a maven on what bothers them; it's why so many stand-up comics can open routines by saying things like, "You know what I hate?" Everybody knows what they hate and can describe it in as much detail as their linguistic capacities will allow. Hillel takes that knob of displeasure and makes it the basis of his ethics. "Do not do what is hateful to you" takes us immediately to a nexus of kvetch, a nodal point where your aversion comes together with your fellow's, and on which the whole idea pivots. Hillel is telling us to put that kvetch to work for us, to proceed from certainty rather than supposition, and begin by refraining from what hurts us or what we dislike or what causes us pain: if you don't like to have your own toe stepped on, don't step on anybody else's; should they *want* you to do so, they'll probably be quick to tell you. Hillel is putting forward an approach that might be called preventative ethics, an ethics designed to minimize strife and misunderstanding by reducing the size and number of potential problem areas.

The beauty, indeed the genius, of Hillel's idea is that it allows us what Christianity would call our fallen state; it lets us start acting like *mentshn* right now. It takes the egotism that has been with us since Adam and Eve and makes it work for, rather than against, us and our development as human beings.

By doing exactly what most moralists are always telling us not to do—thinking of ourselves—we become paradoxically able to start considering others and doing things that benefit them as well as us.

This is the beginning of *mentsh*-hood. You have to go beyond sympathy for another person, even beyond empathy, and on to real identification. Rather than simply imagining yourself in their position, you imagine a complete reversal of positions: you give them your choices, your power, your ability, and you assume theirs. *Then* you decide how you might want to act toward them. You put yourself aside, get as far inside the skin of the other person as you can (we all know that you'll never be able to go all the way), then figure out what's wrong with your original solution and zero in on possible causes for complaint. You identify any grounds for kvetching and do your best to rectify or eliminate them in advance. Rather than doing to someone else that which you'd have them do unto you, you are—by gradually eliminating all the negative and unacceptable courses of action—doing what *they* would have you do to them. And that, of course, is the object of the whole exercise: treating other people *as well* as you treat yourself, not necessarily *as* you treat yourself.

Without the capacity to do this, the commandment to love our neighbor as ourselves is not really intelligible. If, however, we engage in this kind of imaginative sympathy often enough, we'll come to understand others better and better, make fewer and fewer mistakes in interpersonal relations, and be better able to avoid being victimized by *shmucks*.

Isn't this still pretty much what Jesus says, though? And if it is, then what makes it so all-fire Jewish? Jesus mentions the so-called Golden Rule twice in the Gospels, once in Matthew and again in Luke. In the Revised Standard Version of the New Testament, the passages are as follows: "So whatever you wish that men would do to you, do so to them; for this is the law and the prophets" (Matt. 7:12); "And as you wish that men would do to you, do so to them" (Luke 6:31). The version in Matthew is clearly a paraphrase of Hillel's statement, right down to the comment about the law and the prophets. Does the difference in approach, the difference between "do" and "don't do," really make that much of a difference?

In many day-to-day situations, the answer is no. Either one will get you to hold the door open for the lady with all the packages or the gentleman with the walker. Either will teach you to say "please" and "thank you," or remind you to send a salami to your boy in the army. The difference makes itself felt in bigger things, larger issues that go beyond simple courtesy or physical help. Imagine, for instance, that you're depressed. You've lost your job and are working as a telemarketer; your spouse has divorced you and taken the kids, whom you can now see for no longer than an hour at a time and only under supervision at nine A.M. on alternate Sundays. You had to sell your collection of Charlie Parker bootleg acetates to help cover your legal bills, and the rest of your vast jazz collection followed soon afterward. You're forty-five years old and living from paycheck to paycheck, when you're working at all—and the minimum wage that you're earning doesn't even cover your basic expenses. You have no organic illness, no history of emotional problems; it's just that your life has turned to crap and it's really bumming you out.

A friend of yours went through something similar a few

years ago and is eager to help. He's back on his feet now; he's got a new job and a new relationship, his kids have even petitioned the judge to grant him increased access time. Things had been bad, though, as bad as they are for you. He's coming over tonight and has promised to tell you how he was able to cope, how he got through all of this and came out okay.

Good as his word, he turns up. Better than his word, he's got a small package, nicely gift-wrapped, that he hands to you. "Here it is," he says, "the only things that kept me sane."

You open the package eagerly. This is the closest thing you've seen to a present in who knows how long. There's a card on top with an encouraging message, you pull away the last of the wrapping paper, and there they are, two boxed CD sets, brand-new and still in their shrinkwrap. "Here you go," he says. "I'm pretty sure they'll do you as much good as they did me. I really hope so." A tear wells up in one of his eyes.

You look down and there they still are: *Barry Manilow's Greatest Hits, Vols. 1, 2, and 3*, and *Troubadour*, a two-disc boxed set of Donovan's greatest works. You think you're going to puke. Maybe you'll burst into tears, or into the mad laughter of a woman who goes to traffic court and finds herself shunted off to the gallows.

"Why don't we put 'Mandy' on and think about the kids?"

You want to scream, you want to yell, you want to kick your well-meaning friend in such a way as to make future children impossible. Instead, you sit there and listen to "Mandy." And "Atlantis." And even "Jennifer Juniper." And Jennifer is your name.

Your friend meant well. You know it, even though you're feeling even worse than you were before. He knows your taste in music, but he did for you what somebody, as it turns out, had done for him. And for him, it worked. So tonight he started with himself and extrapolated to you. He should at some point have asked, "Is this really the right time to try to broaden a friend's musical horizons? Had someone brought me a bunch of operas in my hour of need, how would that have made me feel?" But he didn't. He brought what *he* would have wanted.

Pretty trivial, no? Take it one notch higher and see what happens, though: a group of missionaries who know what's best for you. There isn't a man or woman among them who doesn't consider Jesus the greatest gift that they've ever received, and they're determined to make a gift of him to you, too, whether you really want him or not. The one thing that they themselves would want more than anything else on earth is to be saved, and now that they have been, they'd like to see you saved, too. Imagine that they run the government, imagine that anybody who turns down this gift will have to leave the country; her belongings will stay, but she will have to go. And she is you. The gift they have is so great and is going to make you so happy that they know that once you've agreed to accept it, you'll thank them for having been so remorseless in their efforts to get you to take it. After all, you *were* unwilling. And now, if you'd just step onto the pyre . . .

It didn't happen every day, it didn't happen everywhere, but it still happened. Hillel's idea wouldn't allow it to happen.

VI

NOT ALL JEWS listen to Hillel any more than all Christians want to convert the rest of the world to Christianity. Hillel, however, claimed that his principle was also the basic principle of his religious faith, and later commentators, Rashi among them, have explained the negative turn of phrase by pointing out that while we're massively capable of doing things that anger God, there's little we can do to help Him. In Jewish terms, the idea of treating God the way we'd like to be treated ourselves is both heretical and silly. Rashi takes the word that is usually translated as "fellow" literally and understands it as "friend." Our friend is God, and Rashi manages to get Hillel's statement to mean that we should go out and learn what God hates and then avoid it.

Less pietistic opinion holds that the main thing that Hillel is saying here is that morality and ethics precede halacha. Yet the story about Hillel and the potential convert might not be quite as straightforward as it appears at first sight. The heathen who comes to Shammai is one of a number of heathens who ask Shammai to convert them and who end up being chased away. In this case, the man says that he will become Jewish if Shammai can teach him the whole Torah, which Shammai seems to understand as Torah in the sense of a scroll containing the five books of Moses, while he, the heathen, stands on one foot. Shammai, who is quoted as saying, "Receive everybody with a cheerful countenance" (*Ovos* 1:15), but is nowhere recorded as having said, "Do as I say, not as I do," says nothing. Instead, he pushes the heathen away with the measuring rod that he's holding.

The heathen then goes to Hillel, who appears to understand Torah in its wider, less confessionally oriented sense of "law, teaching, doctrine." Hillel converts him and then utters his famous sentence. When Hillel characterizes it as "the whole of

the Torah in its entirety"—think of Torah as a one-word version of Keats's "all ye know on earth and all ye need to know"—
there is certainly a dig at Shammai here, an implied command
to the inquirer to forget about that man who was threatening
you with his yardstick; the real Torah is about those things that
have no limits to their measure, and he clearly got none of it
from Shammai.

Note also that Hillel's rule is fulfilled almost as soon as it is
revealed. "Don't do to others," he tells the proselyte, and then,
"Go, learn." It's a subtle but unmistakable way of letting the
ex-heathen know that the interview is over. "How would you
like it if people kept barging in on you with smart-ass questions? You wanted an answer, you got it. Now go do something
with it." Of course, Hillel doesn't make a big deal about it, just
sneaks it quietly by without ever ruffling the smile on his face.

Hillel is no Kris Kringle or Casper the Friendly Ghost, nor
do you have to be one if you want to be a *mentsh*. There's a
difference between a good person and a Goody Two-shoes. A
mentsh is accommodating, but is never a sap; a *mentsh* can
get annoyed, but won't become annoying. A *mentsh* is a real
person who lives in a real world, where he spends far too much
time dealing with *shmucks* while fighting not to become one
himself. He's smart, tough, worldly, and honest. Remember,
Hillel was Hillel when he was still chopping wood and nobody
was asking him for anything but kindling. Raymond Chandler's description of his ideal detective—of Philip Marlowe,
really—might be a bit idealized, but it certainly hits all the
main points, except for the all-important fact that he can just
as easily be she:

He must be a complete man and a common and yet an unusual man. He must be, to use a rather weathered phrase, a
man of honor—by instinct, by inevitability, without thought
of it, and certainly without saying. He must be the best man
in his world and a good enough man for any world. I do not
care much about his private life; he is neither a eunuch nor
a satyr; I think he might seduce a duchess and I am quite
sure he would not spoil a virgin; if he is a man of honor
in one thing, he is that in all things. . . . [He has] a disgust
for sham, and a contempt for pettiness. . . . If there were
enough like him, the world would be a very safe place to
live in, without becoming too dull to be worth living in.

Like Hillel in his ancient robes, like all those detectives who
wear wide-brimmed hats, call most women "dames," and spend
their time solving murders, a *mentsh* never forgets that actions
have consequences: farther down on the same page of tractate
Shabbos, the three heathens whom Shammai chased away and
who were then converted by Hillel come together sometime later
and say, "Shammai's bad temper sought to drive us from the
world, but Hillel's mild humility brought us under the wings of
the divine presence" (*Shabbos* 31a). They are not the same people
as they would have been had Hillel acted differently.

Important as brains are, there is also the matter of sensibil-
ity. What is an aspiring detecto-*mentsh* to do if he or she isn't
as smart as Philip Marlowe? What if you're a little understaffed
in the *seykhl* department? Take a look at P. G. Wodehouse and
never forget: Bertie Wooster, *mentsh*; Gussie Fink-Nottle, newt
fancier, *shmuck*.

VII

HILLEL'S MAXIM IS basically the how-to manual for the commandment in Leviticus about loving your neighbor, a sover-
eign remedy for the kind of exceptionalism that can always
find an excuse for yourself while denying one to everybody else.
There's a phrase in the Talmud (*Pesokhim* 113a) that's become
the basis of a Yiddish proverb: "*Ven freyt zikh got?* When does
God rejoice? *Az an oreman gefint a metsiye un git zi op*, when
a poor person finds something that's been lost and returns it to
its owner." Despite the fact that the pauper could either use the
item or sell it for some much-needed money, he does the honest
thing, the right thing. By thinking, "How would I feel if somebody stole this from me after I'd misplaced it?" instead of "My
need is greater than the owner's, so I have a right to keep this
and dispose of it in any way that I see fit," he doesn't make himself any less poor, but he's certainly made everyone around him
a little more rich. In such a way of thinking, all egos become
equal; none is any higher or lower than your own.

This kind of ethical egalitarianism helps to keep people
from succumbing to the temptation to turn into the worst
kind of *shmuck*, the kind who works actively to oppress
others. In his book *The Lucifer Effect*, Philip Zimbardo describes an experiment carried out by an elementary school
teacher who wanted to teach her students about racial preju-
dice "by arbitrarily relating the eye color of children in her
classroom to high or low status. When those with blue eyes
were associated with privilege, they readily assumed a dom-
inant role over their brown-eyed peers, even abusing them

verbally and physically." The kids in the privileged group immediately began to perform better in school, while the kids in the other group did worse.

The next day, though,

Mrs. Elliott told the class she had erred. In fact, the opposite was true: brown eyes were better than blue eyes! Here was the chance for the brown-eyed children, who had experienced the negative impact of being discriminated against, to show compassion now that they were on top of the heap . . . [but] the brown-eyes gave what they got. They dominated, they discriminated, and they abused their former blue-eyed abusers.

This isn't Bosnia or Rwanda; these are eight-year-olds in Iowa who haven't the ghost of a pretext to go after each other. Without some way of checking their egos, though, something to keep them from doing cruel and obnoxious things only because they can, the kids, like so many adults before them, simply fall into a pattern of reciprocal abuse that has no other motive than opportunity.

"Do unto others" doesn't really cut it once you've dehumanized those others and reduced them to something less than you are. You're better off to shift your focus away from them and back to yourself. If you act enough like Hillel to bring your aversion to being a *shmuck* to the fore, you will refuse to do things to others that you don't want done to yourself, regardless of what color their eyes are or how little you might think of them. You'll be able to overcome any desire for revenge, any need to show someone who's boss or what's what. You don't have to like them, you don't even have to hate them. All that matters is that you aren't them.

VIII

HILLEL LETS THE new convert know quite explicitly that even though "Do not do what is hateful to you to your fellow" can be said to sum up the whole of the Torah, there is still plenty of commentary that he's going to have to learn, myriad different ways to make himself not hateful. The importance of study in Judaism has always been seen as a lovely, wonderful thing that let Jews sharpen their minds instead of their swords, gave them a certain advantage over their less studious neighbors when it came to quick thinking, and prepared us all for nice professional positions that keep us from getting our hands dirty. A great deal has been made of the Jewish devotion to study for its own sake, to the acquisition of knowledge and improvement of understanding for no other reason than that all knowledge is felt to be useful and that it's better to be smart than stupid.

Recent research, though, suggests that the idea of "and you shall meditate upon it day and night" might have an inherently moral function completely independent of the sanctity that a Jew who studies the Torah is likely to attribute to the act of studying or the words of the sacred text.

In an experiment to measure hypocrisy, David DeSteno and Piercarlo Valdesolo offered a group of subjects a choice between two tasks, a short and easy one or one that was difficult and long. The subjects were told that they had to assign one of these tasks to themselves and one to a subject from another group (which didn't really exist), who wouldn't be told that the current subject had determined which task he or she would be performing.

The subjects were also told that tossing a coin would be the fairest way to make this decision, and they were supplied with a randomizing computer program that would simulate an actual coin-toss. Ninety-two percent immediately took the easy task for themselves; 8 percent used the randomizer. No participants assigned themselves the difficult task. Those who had used the randomizer were then eliminated from the group and the rest were asked to evaluate their actions for fairness. On a scale of 1 to 7, the average score fell well past the midpoint.

A different group was then assigned to watch others assign themselves the easy job and then rate them for fairness on the same scale. The observers' fairness ratings were significantly lower than those of the first group.

Two more groups were then arbitrarily divided into sub-groups based on the color of randomly distributed wristbands and then asked to evaluate the fairness of "participants" from either group who assigned themselves the easy task. The results were comparable to those from the first round, except that participants whose wristbands were the same color as the evaluators' received even higher mean fairness ratings than the unaffiliated individuals had, and members of the other groups ranked lower than the people evaluated in the second group.

With this experiment, DeSteno and Valdesolo have confirmed many of our less rosy notions of human nature. "A person finds no fault with himself," as it says (*Kesubos* 105b), and we now have a more accurate measure of how shameless people can be about applying one standard to themselves (and members of their group) and another to the rest of the world.

Things got even more interesting when they repeated the experiment, but with one slight difference: the addition of what is called a "cognitive constraint," a mental task intended to divide or deflect the participant's attention. Before answering the questions about fairness in assigning tasks, the participants were given a mental job to do. As the experimenters describe it:

Participants were told that the experimenters were interested in how people make judgments when they are distracted. To simulate distraction, they would be asked to remember a string of digits at the same time that they were responding to a series of questions. Participants were told that a string of seven digits would appear on the screen before each question. They would then have to answer the question within 10 seconds, immediately after which they would have to recall the digit string that had preceded the question. Participants were also told that it was extremely important to provide the most accurate answers possible for questions comprising the assignment evaluation measure.

The participants were thinking about the numbers rather than themselves. The cognitive constraint "resulted in the disappearance of the hypocrisy effect; participants experiencing load judged their own transgressions to be as unfair as the same behavior when enacted by another." In other words, they were so busy trying to remember the numbers that they were unable to come up with any exculpatory bullshit. They didn't actually *behave* any better than they did in the first experiment; they still gave themselves the easy job without regard for fairness to the next participant, but at least they got to a point where they were willing to acknowledge that they were behaving like *shmucks*. It might not be much, but it's a start.

The findings of Valdesolo and DeSteno might lend a more functional or utilitarian cast to the long-standing Jewish emphasis on study. If the Torah never really departs from our mouths and we meditate on it day and night, as the book of Joshua tells us to do (and the word translated as "meditate" can also mean "speak, utter, recite"); if we set the Lord before us always (see Psalms 16:8), perhaps what we're really doing is employing a religiously or community-mandated cognitive constraint that, even if it can't keep us from doing the wrong thing, at least makes it more difficult for us to rationalize our wrongdoing. "Woe unto those," says Isaiah, "who call evil good and good evil, who make darkness into light and light into darkness" (Isa. 5:20). We've come almost full circle: by thinking about something other than ourselves—whether it's the glory of the Lord or a randomly generated string of numbers—we become able to see ourselves as we are.

Such an understanding of the purpose of constant study might help to explain some of the more troubling rabbinic pronouncements about what happens to those who aren't paying attention:

> Rabbi Jacob says: If somebody is walking along the road studying, but breaks off to say, "How beautiful is this tree, how beautiful is this field"—Scripture considers him guilty against himself.
>
> (OVOS 3:7)

"Guilty against himself" means "has put himself into a position in which he is liable to lose his life." While Rabbi Jacob is alluding in part to the folk belief that no harm can come to a person while he is engaged in Torah study—or no harm from the kinds of demons who frequent roads and trails; brigands might be another question—the basic thrust of his comment, that leaving off study on account of any distraction is a capital sin, has troubled students and commentators for a very long time: you look at a tree or a field that's just been plowed and you could die? *Vos far a meshigas*, what kind of meshugass, is that? What happens if you look at a tree *in* a field that's just been plowed, and appreciate the entire scene? Will you die slower? Or sooner? And if you keep your eyes closed and hire a little child to lead you, are you gonna live forever?

If we recall that Torah scrolls tended not to be owned by individuals and that the so-called Oral Law (a term that seems to have been introduced by our old friend Hillel) really was oral for a very long time, that is, was not written down at all, the idea of studying while walking around and repeating things to yourself as if you were learning a part in a play does not sound quite so outlandish. Trees, fields, wistful vistas become no more than the wallpaper of the world: pleasant, necessary even, but background, nothing but background. Whatever you're reviewing in your mind acts like Valdesolo and De-Steno's string of numbers; it takes up just enough of your attention to keep you from injecting yourself into the scene before you. If, however, you drop the cognitive load that you've been *shlepping* along with you and suddenly project yourself (and your self) back into the surroundings, in which you now have an interest, you've reverted to a frame of mind in which you're happy to make excuses for yourself that you would never allow for anyone else.

Up until surprisingly recently, books were expensive and not always easy to come by, and you couldn't always count on being able to get hold of the one you needed when you needed it. Considerably more emphasis was therefore placed on memorization than is fashionable today; as recently as 1939, the ability to recite two hundred folios (four hundred very large pages) of Talmud from memory (and prove that you understood them) was the prerequisite for the entrance examinations for Chachmei Lublin, the Lublin yeshiva often characterized as the Harvard of the prewar yeshiva world. Those who couldn't muster the requisite four hundred pages from memory weren't even eligible to fail. I have been told that students admitted to the yeshiva memorized a further folio every day. While four hundred pages is an exceptional amount, the principle here is the same as it is in elementary school: you can't get rid of this stuff—and God knows, generations of ex-yeshiva boys have tried. Twenty-four hours a day, it never leaves your mind, even if it isn't always coming out of your mouth—and traditional study still has a very strong oral component.

It isn't like this stuff is easy to understand; there's a lot of cognitive constraint going on there. You can't study twenty-four hours a day, but you can spend enough time thinking about something that is not you, that might have no direct bearing on your life—as we mentioned earlier, much of the Bible is about how to build tabernacles and offer sacrifices that none of us is ever going to see—to be able to step back and see your own behavior for what it really is. The daily study preferred by traditional Judaism is more than a means of acquiring information or strengthening your sense of belonging to the group; it serves as a constraint against cutting yourself any more slack than is cut for anybody else. It makes you aware of the all-important fact that refusing to make exceptions—especially for yourself or the members of your own little group—is the basis of all morality.

Hillel's dictum strengthens this anti-exceptionalism by forcing you to judge everyone else by the standards you'd use for yourself. The leniency you'd grant yourself is automatically extended to others because you are forced to treat them just as you'd treat yourself. True, the use of the cognitive constraint only affects the accuracy and honesty of the way in which you assess your behavior, rather than the behavior itself, but the ability to remove the spectacles of self-interest and see your behavior for what it really is, is the first step to change. All education can thus be used as an occasion for *mentsh*-hood, as a path up from *shmuckery*.

IX

IF YOU FIND yourself saying, "I sure acted like a *shmuck*" often enough, you might eventually be moved to do something about it. But how often do you have to tell yourself what a *shmuck* you've been before you stop being one? How much time might elapse between that first tentative realization that you're not really the life of the party, the office clown, Hugh Hefner Jr., or the Lord Jehovah's security guard, and a decision to do something about it that doesn't consist of trying even harder?

Recognizing the fact that you are a *shmuck* and learning how to stop being one if you've never been prodded by memories of Hebrew school or heard of any of the people mentioned in these pages, are what Harold Ramis's film, *Groundhog Day*, is all about. I can't improve on Roger Ebert's summary:

> The movie, as everyone knows, is about a·man who finds himself living the same day over and over and over again. He is the only person in his world who knows this is happening, and after going through periods of dismay and bitterness, revolt and despair, suicidal self-destruction and cynical recklessness, he begins to do something that is alien to his nature. He begins to learn.

Watching the movie, we see how Phil Connors, a *shmuck* of a TV weatherman played by Bill Murray, gradually begins the learning that Ebert mentions. It is never explained why he is stuck so tightly in February 2 that he can kill himself one day and then wake up on the morning of the same day on which he killed himself and live it all over again. He can live or die as he chooses, but he'll be waking up at 6 A.M., with the clock radio in his room playing "I Got You, Babe" by Sonny and Cher, to face the same twenty-four hours once more.

We never find out how many February 2's he lives through—an early draft of the script has him reading through the entire Punxsutawney public library at the rate of one page a day, though the film as released doesn't have quite that sense of Indian epic time—but he's there long enough to go from absolute beginner at the piano to being an accomplished-enough player to be able to get through a bit of Rachmaninoff and some credible light jazz by the end, and he doesn't start taking piano lessons until the movie is nearly over.

Connors has the hots for his producer, Rita (played by Andie MacDowell), and since he's the only character who re-members all the different February 2's, he begins feeling her out for information about herself that he can use the next day to show how much they have in common. He memorizes French poetry, orders sweet vermouth (with a twist, yet) to show that he shares her tastes, asks her heartfelt questions about what she wants out of life. Connors eventually gets her back to his bed and breakfast but, after Rita tells him that she won't sleep with him that night, unleashes his full *shmuck* self in a desperate attempt to score and tells Rita that he loves her. Rita, who has no recollection of the dozen or two February 2's that have led up to this moment, looks at him as if he'd just slapped her and says, "You don't even know me. . . . This whole day was just one long setup!"

Faced with an eternity of frustration, Connors gets even more depressed and tries to kill himself at various times and in various ways, sometimes with the groundhog, sometimes with somebody else, sometimes all by himself, only to wake right back up at 6 A.M. to another Groundhog Day. He tells Rita that he must be some sort of god, since he's unkillable; he demonstrates his local omniscience for her, telling her all about the lives of the other people in the diner where they're having this conversation, and even predicting a few minor events just before they happen. "I told you!" he tells her when she asks, yet again, how he does it. "I wake up every day right here, right in Punxsutawney, and it's always February second and I can't turn it off." He fills Rita in on the details of their shared Groundhog Day past, and she proposes staying up all night with him, as a sort of "objective witness" to what's been happening. They stay up all night, and just before six, as Rita is dozing off, Phil admits that he loves her: "I don't deserve someone like you, but if I ever would, I swear I would love you for the rest of my life." Rita wishes him good night.

The alarm sounds, it's another Groundhog Day, but Phil has found his cognitive constraint—Rita, who is distracting enough to force him into accurate self-assessment—and after years' worth of Groundhog Days he figures out Hillel's idea for himself. He shows up for that morning's report on Groundhog Day with coffee for Rita and the cameraman; he hears some Mozart that he likes and immediately starts taking piano lessons; he starts to look after the aged bum whom he used to walk by every day. Since it's a small town and he's been there for so long that he knows everything that's going to happen, he starts to prevent bad things from happening: keeps a little girl from being run over; walks into a restaurant, goes directly to a table where he administers the Heimlich maneuver to a choking man; catches a boy as he falls out of a tree. Rita is finally won over. They spend the night together and wake up on February 3.

The turning point occurs when Phil realizes that even though he can't get out of February 2, he can change things in such a way that he might have a chance of getting Rita to love him. All that needs to be changed is Phil, and he sets about doing so. Things move quickly past Rita, though, and Phil begins to take an active role in the lives of many of the townspeople, thanks in large part to the imaginative sympathy that is so important a part of Hillel's idea. In view of the circumstances, there is really nothing that anybody in Punxsutawney can do for Phil. He isn't helping them because that's how he'd want them to treat him, he's helping them because helping them is the right thing to do, because—corny as it sounds—being nice to all those people makes the town, which is all the world that Connors has anymore, a nicer place for everybody. In one of the extras that come with the DVD version of the movie, Danny Rubin, who came up with the original idea and then wrote the script, says that the movie is about "doing what you can do in the moment to make things better instead of making them worse." Which might not sound like very much, but it's just about all you can do in life.

X

THE PATH FROM Hillel to Phil Connors bears out yet another piece of the Talmud's psychology, probably one of the deepest observations in all of its thirty-six tractates:

> Let a person always occupy himself with Torah and good
> deeds, even if he isn't doing them for their own sake; for
> from doing them with an ulterior motive, he will come to
> do them for their own sake.
>
> (NOZIR 23B)

This, of course, is exactly what happens with Phil. He might not be studying any Torah, but he certainly occupies himself with good deeds. His initial efforts at treating others with some semblance of dignity and respect are either attempts to relieve the tedium of always waking up to the same damned day or aspects of his unsuccessful campaign to get into Rita's pants. Eventually, though, his ulterior motives recede and then vanish altogether, and he is left with the skills that he had to teach himself in order to look like the kind of man that Rita would want. Instead of messing with people because he can, instead of looking for opportunities to *get away* with things, Phil now begins to seek out opportunities to *give away* the things that the people around him need: help, consideration, advice, even money.

Connors is still doing things because he can, but the "because" has been redirected from himself to others, and has taken on a new meaning. Where "Because I can" used to be the little devil that sits on Tom Hulce's shoulder at the party in *Animal House* (also co-written by Harold Ramis) and tells him to "Fuck [the girl who's passed out], fuck her brains out," it now means Elwood P. Dowd inviting strangers to join him and Harvey, the six-foot-three invisible rabbit, for martinis at Charlie's Place. Instead of "Fuck you, I'll do what I want," "Because I can" has come to mean, "What can I do to help you?"

For the first three-quarters of the movie, when Phil does nothing except what he feels like—get drunk, get laid, try to commit suicide without coming back to life a few hours later—none of his actions appears to have any consequence: he wakes up at 6 A.M. on Groundhog Day no matter how high a cliff he plunged from the day before or how many bullets tore through his body. He lacks the insight to see that he could make things less tedious and instead acts like a kid who doesn't want to wash because he's only going to get dirty all over again.

And nothing would have changed, he might well have been stuck that way forever, had Rita not led him to see his predicament as an opportunity:

Sometimes I wish I had a thousand lifetimes. One to be a great journalist. One to, I don't know, go back to school, study art, or auto mechanics. One just to take care of all the busywork, you know, pay the bills, get my car tuned up. One to be the wild woman of Borneo. One to be Mother Teresa. Maybe it's not a curse, Phil. It all just depends on how you look at it.

The next February 2, Phil brings her and the cameraman coffee, starts taking music lessons, begins to *do* something. Rita's wish list is all about herself, but once Phil adapts it to himself, it leads him farther and farther out of himself, deeper and deeper into the lives of other people. And all of them, Phil and the others, start to look like they might be happy. Or happier than they were. Thinking about others, really thinking about them and not just pretending, seems to be the best way of advancing yourself and getting what you want. Not only does everybody win, but you save yourself the trouble of ever having to fabricate another excuse for letting somebody down.

"A *mitsve*," my mother would have told me, "*firt tsi a mitsve*, one good deed leads to another good deed, as one transgression does to the next." I don't know if she knew that she was quoting *Ovos* when she said this or if it's just something that she thought she'd always known, but one good turn certainly deserves another in any language. Phil Connors ends up doing a lot of things for a lot of people and not only gets himself out of a horrible rut by doing so, but he manages to get all the stuff that he wanted for himself by doing things for others. Which only proves that the world itself runs on Yiddish-speaking principles: the best way to get what you want and make all those bastards out there so jealous that they'll want to poke their own eyes out is to go out of your way to be nice to those bastards. *That's* the way to show them. *That's* how a *mentsh* gets revenge.

Notes

THREE: *Extending the* Shmuck

64 **"Stiffed us . . . for the helicopter bill":** http://www.thirteen.org/scienceandnature/ethics-criminals-and-mt-everest-panel-discussion, retrieved October 30, 2008.

FOUR: *What a* Mentsh *Does*

107 **"Rabbi Leib Dimimles":** Louis I. Newman, *The Hasidic Anthology*, p. 127.

116 **Yekhiel-Meir of Gostynin:** Y. K. Kadish, *Siakh Sarfey Koydesh*, vol. 2, p. 103.

116 **A better Hasidic story:** Ibid., p. 104.

116 **Almost as sartorial:** Martin Buber, *Tales of the Hasidim*, vol. 1, p. 128.

117 **"Justice, justice":** Kadish, *Siakh Sarfey Koydesh*, vol. 1, p. 129.

119 **"His wife was meeting him":** *The Apartment*, screenplay on IMDB, http://www.imsdb.com/scripts/Apartment,-The.html.

121 **"Dr. Dreyfuss: I don't know":** Ibid. I've omitted stage directions, preserved original spelling of *mentsh*, and the typo in its second occurrence.

125 **"[The Baal Shem Tov]":** A. J. Heschel, *Kotsk: In Gerangl far Emesdikayt*, p. 37.

125 **"*Derekh erets*, good manners":** Y. Y. Artan, *Sefer Emes ve-Emunoh*, p. 44.

127 **"There is a line":** Heschel, *Kotsk*, p. 34.

FIVE: *How to Do It Like a* Mentsh

136 **"Two neighbours came":** Joseph Jacobs, *"The Fables of Aesop"*; retrieved online at http://mythfolklore.net/aesopica/jacobs/54.htm.

141 **There's a story:** B. Parnes (Mordkhe Mishkin), *Fun der rabonisher velt*, pp. 53–54.

144 **"A poor man asked":** Louis I. Newman, *The Hasidic Anthology*, pp. 438–39.

149 **"There are exceptions to rules":** Lawrence Kohlberg, *Essays on Moral Development, Vol. I: The Philosophy of Moral Development*, p. 39.

162 **"He must be a complete man":** Raymond Chandler, "The Simple Art of Murder," in *The Simple Art of Murder*, pp. 20–21.

163 **"By arbitrarily relating":** Philip Zimbardo, *The Lucifer Effect*, p. 144.

164 **"Mrs. Elliott told her class":** Ibid.

165 **In an experiment to measure hypocrisy:** All information on this experiment is taken from Piercarlo Valdesolo and David DeSteno, "Moral Hypocrisy: Social Groups and the Flexibility of Virtue," *Psychological Science* 18 (2007): 689–90.

167 **"Participants were told":** All quotations and information on this experiment from Piercarlo Valdesolo and David DeSteno, "The Duality of Virtue: Deconstructing the Moral Hypocrite," *Journal of Experimental Social Psychology* 44(5)(2008): 1334–38.

172 **"The movie, as everyone knows":** Roger Ebert, Review of *Groundhog Day*, at http://rogerebert.suntimes.com/apps/pbcs.dll/article?AID=/20050130/REVIEWS08/501300301/1023.

Bibliography

Artan, Y. Y. *Sefer Emes ve-Emunoh.* Jerusalem: no publisher, 1972.

Bernstein, Ignaz. *Jüdische Sprichwörter und Redensarten* (rpt). Hildesheim: Georg Olms, 1969.

Buber, Martin. *Tales of the Hasidim.* Two volumes. New York: Schocken, 1947–1948.

Chandler, Raymond. *The Simple Art of Murder.* New York: Ballantine Books, 1980.

Ebert, Roger. Review of *Groundhog Day.* Rogerebert.com. December 28, 2008. http://rogerebert.suntimes.com/apps/pbcs.dll/article?AID=/200 50130/REVIEWS08/501300301/1023.

"Ethics, Criminals and Mt. Everest Panel Discussion." *Thirteen WNET New York.* October 30, 2008. http://www.thirteen.org/scienceandnature/ethics-criminals-and-mt-everest-panel-discussion.

"Excerpts Paint a Sordid Picture." *Globe and Mail*, December 10, 2008, A14.

Heschel, A. J. *Kotsk: In Gerangl far Emesdikayt.* Tel Aviv: ha-Menora, 1973.

Jacobs, Joseph. "The Fables of Aesop." *Aesopica: Aesop's Fables in English, Latin & Greek.* October 12, 2008. http://mythfolklore.net/aesopica/jacobs/54.htm.

Kadish, Y. K. *Siakh Sarfey Koydesh.* Three volumes. Bnai Brak: Gitler Brothers, 1989.

Kane, George, and E. Talbot Donaldson, eds. *Piers Plowman: The B version; Will's visions of Piers Plowman, do-well, do better and do-best.* London: Athlone Press, 1975.

Kohlberg, Lawrence. *The Philosophy of Moral Development: Moral Stages and the Idea of Justice.* San Francisco: Harper & Row, 1981.

Newman, Louis I. *The Hasidic Anthology.* New York: Schocken, 1963.

Parnes, B. (pseud., Mishkin, Mordkhe). *Fun der rabonisher velt.* New York: Star Hebrew Book Company, 1928.

Roth, Cecil, ed. *The Dark Ages: Jews in Christian Europe, 711–1096.* New Brunswick, N.J.: Rutgers University Press, 1966.

Valdesolo, Piercarlo, and David DeSteno. "Moral Hypocrisy: Social Groups and the Flexibility of Virtue." *Psychological Science* 18(2007): 689–90.

———. "The Duality of Virtue: Deconstructing the Moral Hypocrite." *Journal of Experimental Social Psychology* 44(5)(2008): 1334–38.

Weinreich, Maks. *Di Geshikhte fun der Yidisher Shprakh.* Four volumes. New York: Yidisher Visnshaftlikher Institut, 1973.

Wilder, Billy, and I. A. L. Diamond. *The Apartment.* The Internet Movie Script Database (IMSDb). January 2, 2009. http://www.imsdb.com/scripts/Apartment,-The.html.

Zborowski, Mark, and Elizabeth Herzog. *Life Is with People: The Culture of the Shtetl.* New York: Schocken, 1971.

Zimbardo, Philip. *The Lucifer Effect.* New York: Random House, 2008.

Index

Insights,
Interviews
& More . . .

Meet Michael Wex

Suzanne McLaren

> I was born in Lethbridge, Alberta, the first city of any size on the Canadian side of the border with Montana, moved from there to Calgary, from Calgary to Toronto, then back to Calgary, and once more to Toronto—all before I finished high school. I spoke Yiddish with my parents, grandparents, shopkeepers, oldsters, synagogue-goers, and every rabbi I encountered, without really giving it a second thought until I was more or less grown-up. The ability to get through a Yiddish newspaper or novel with no more difficulty than an English one was simply a fringe benefit of a Hebrew religious education, and just as I never studied Yiddish in school, I never could have imagined putting it to any serious

66 I never could have imagined putting [Yiddish] to any serious use in later life.... Speaking Yiddish to anyone my own age was the high road to endless celibacy. **99**

use in later life. There was no such thing as a Yiddish career, no way of using Yiddish to get myself a girlfriend. Speaking Yiddish to anyone my own age was the high road to endless celibacy, nearly as fatal to fulfillment as speaking Yiddish with the parents of any girl whom I liked; no sane girl wants to kiss a guy whom her parents admire because he's so Jewish.

After a few too many such incidents, I kept my Yiddish private until I found myself in graduate school at the University of Toronto. The pervasive anti-Semitism of the medieval literature that I was studying, not to mention the large number of devout Catholics in my department, brought the Yiddish back out of me in a big way, and after a mere six years of doctoral studies—the job market was so bad that I was afraid of *not* being able to spend thirty-five or forty years droning on about Chaucer— I abandoned Christian allegory, returned to Yiddish, and learned the meaning of the term "semi-employed."

Though I've taught on contract at the University of Toronto and the University of Michigan, most of the jobs I've held for the last twenty years or so had nothing to do with Yiddish. Three years as a research associate in neurosurgery— thank God for on-the-job training—were followed by menial office jobs and more casual labor than I care to remember.

Little of interest developed from anything that I learned after my bar mitzvah. I'd started doing stand-up and storytelling while still in graduate school and used these to supplement whatever ▶

I could earn in Yiddish. When I wasn't teaching Yiddish privately or lecturing on it in public, I was translating it into English; when I wasn't doing that, I was translating English into Yiddish for anyone who was willing to pay: I even translated Weill and Brecht's *Threepenny Opera* from German into Yiddish for a production that was mounted in Montreal.

I published a novel called *Shlepping the Exile* about an orthodox, Yiddish-speaking teenager living in southern Alberta in 1956 (I was born in 1954, which should give you some idea of the book's autobiographical content), adapted it into a full-length performance piece, then went on to write a series of other stage shows based on different aspects of Yiddish culture, each one a delightful mélange of dramatic monologue, stand-up comedy, and the Babylonian Talmud. The German bassist and composer Heiko Lehmann wrote music for all of them and collaborated with me on original Yiddish songs. Our most successful piece, *I Just Wanna Jewify*, takes the operas of Richard Wagner back to their imaginary Yiddish roots. It's the only one that has never been performed in German.

I live in Toronto with my wife and daughter. ∾

For more information about Michael Wex and his books, please visit his Web site at www.michaelwex.com.

66 [I] adapted [my novel] into a full-length performance piece, then went on to write a series of other stage shows based on different aspects of Yiddish culture, each one a delightful mélange of dramatic monlogue, stand-up comedy, and the Babylonian Talmud. 99

I Forgot the Most Important Part

HOWEVER I MIGHT CHOOSE to describe the book in interviews or essays, *How to Be a Mentsh (and Not a Shmuck)* is really the published counterpart of the errands that I too often run without a list. I come home loaded down with stuff—newspapers, butch wax, a three-pack of new cholent-flavored Pez (a candy once forbidden to many Jewish children; it originated in Austria, where its name—properly pronounced *pets*—cannot be distinguished from the plural of the Yiddish *putz*), a perfectly good eight-track player that some idiot put out with the garbage, and anything else that happened to catch my eye—everything, that is, except for the lightbulb or toilet paper that drove me out of the house in the first place.

The same flawed process is evident in this book. Careful as I was to describe the basic meanings of *mentsh* and *shmuck* and trace the ways in which those meanings developed, I completely forgot to mention the incident that got me thinking about *mentsh*-hood to begin with. I touch on Lefty Frizzell, but leave out the anonymous Hasid who made the whole thing possible.

A couple of weeks before Christmas 2007, I was walking down Fifth Avenue in New York around five on a rotten afternoon. It was windy and sleeting. People on the sidewalk bowed their heads as if they were ashamed to be seen in ▶

such a mess and plowed blindly ahead
from one corner to the next, looking up
only to consult traffic lights or check for
cars. Near the northwest corner of Fifth
and Fifty-first, just past the big H&M,
I noticed a Hasid in the middle of
Fifty-first Street, midway between me
and the green light on the other side.
A girl of ten or eleven, clearly his
daughter, was holding onto his
sleeve as they crossed the street.

A man dressed as Santa Claus was
standing beside a tree just south of
Fifty-first, ringing his bell at Façonnable's
display window and cowering beneath
the sleet. I don't know if he was collecting
for the Sally Anne (Salvation Army) or
for some other charity—the metal stand
with the sign was on the Santa's far
side—but whatever the organization,
he wasn't doing it much good. The
rush hour crowd on Fifth Avenue was
too busy looking at the sidewalk even
to glance in his direction.

I was fifteen or twenty feet behind
the Hasid and his daughter, who came
to a halt once they'd finished crossing
the street. The Hasid hoisted up the
skirts of his long black coat, reached
into his pants pocket, and handed
something to the girl. She looked down
at her hand, then back up at the Hasid.
He nodded. She turned around, walked
over to the Santa, and put the bill in his
kettle. Santa nodded in acknowledgment.
By this time, the Hasid had caught up
to the girl. He nodded to the Santa, said
something, walked over, and shook his

hand. The Santa rang his bell again and the Hasid and his daughter went on their way.

It isn't every day that you see Santa Claus getting money from a Hasid in the middle of a minor ice storm, and I have to say that I was mightily impressed. Not only was the Hasid acting in strict accord with Jewish rules of charity but he was also teaching his daughter to do the same thing. Sending her to the Santa to make a donation answered any possible questions about who deserves to benefit from the largesse of the nondestitute: Everybody. Not just the needy who resemble us or whose beliefs or ways of life meet with our unqualified approval. Poor is poor, and so long as the money won't be used against us by the enemies of Jews and Judaism, we're obliged to give. God will judge them; our job is to help sustain them. *Tsedokeh*, the Hebrew and Yiddish word usually translated as "charity," is nearer in meaning to "righteousness" or "justice"; by giving charity, we're only doing what we're supposed to, only giving others their mandated due. According to the Talmud, such money has always been earmarked for those who are poorer than we are; all we've been doing is holding onto it.

By having his daughter give the money to the Santa rather than doing so himself, he taught her everything just mentioned about this matter-of-fact approach to our duty to others. More, he's taught it viscerally, and not only verbally. ▶

Rather than serve as an example for his daughter, the Hasid lets her become an example for herself. This pious Jewish girl will never walk past another street corner Santa without feeling at least a twinge of obligation. And, though it's out of her hands, she could even become an example to others: if a Hasidic girl can throw money into Santa's kettle, then Santa's fellow-Christians, as well as any other non-Christian passers-by, should be able to figure out that they ought to be doing the same. The Hasid is engaged in the process of turning a child into a *mentsh* who will then be able to make *mentshn* on her own.

I picked up my pace enough to catch up with Hasid and his daughter. "*Antshildikt, Reb Yid*, Excuse me, sir. I saw what you just did . . ." I explained why I felt compelled to stop him. "That was a wonderful thing that you did with the Santa Claus back there. And to give the *mitzvah*"—the good deed and its reward—"to the kid, it's like a double *kiddesh ha-shem*," a twofold way of making God and His Torah look good in public. "You know what, make that a triple *kiddesh ha-shem*."

The Hasid wiped the sleet from his glasses and looked at me like I thought *kiddesh ha-shem*, sanctifying the name of God, was an ice cream sundae. "And what else was I supposed to do?" He shrugged. "*Der urel zol klingen azoy mitn glekl imzist?* The uncircumcised one"—it was his way of denoting the Santa—"should ring his bell for nothing?" He shrugged rhetorically and walked off with his daughter.

That's the sort of thing that I hope this book will inspire in its readers, the knowledge that when Santa Claus rings his bell, he's tolling for thee.

And now I'm going to go squeeze some Charmin. ∽

Ten Rules of Thumb for Everyday Life

Five Signs That You're a *Shmuck*

You're a *shmuck* if . . .

1. You know that you're great because your mother would never lie to you.
2. Someone else is always responsible for your failure to do what you're supposed to do.
3. You don't understand what's wrong with receiving envelopes full of cash from a known felon.
4. You send your life coach to tell your spouse that you want a divorce.
5. You have a life coach instead of a conscience.

Five Signs That You're a *Mentsh*

You're a *mentsh* if . . .

1. You know that just because something isn't "wrong," it isn't necessarily right.
2. You cut everybody else the same slack as you cut for yourself.
3. You remember that everybody else—including the people in front of you in line—is just as important as you are.
4. You do the right thing, even when no one is looking and no one will ever know.
5. You don't treat others the way you don't want them to treat you. ∾

The Best-Known *Shmuck* in the World?

I'M OFTEN ASKED FOR LISTS of *mentshn* and *shmucks*, both contemporary and historical. Sometimes, I'm even asked to pronounce judgment on living celebrities and politicians. It's not unusual for interviewers or people at Q&A sessions following a reading to come out with things like, "Obama—*mentsh* or *shmuck*?" or "I think Lady Gaga's a *mentsh* but my boyfriend says she's a *shmuck*. Which of us is right?"

I'm not going to answer these questions here, either; life is difficult enough, and I try to avoid libel suits and death threats that aren't absolutely necessary. Instead, I prefer to use fictional personages, characters from literature, movies, television, and the stage. It's a fun game to play, either alone or with friends, and could actually lead to some thought about the nature of *mentsh*-hood instead of screaming and fisticuffs. Give it a try. Here's a little sample to get you started.

Five Famous Fictional *Mentshn*

1. Philip Marlowe
2. Bertie Wooster
3. Rick Blaine (as played by Humphrey Bogart in *Casablanca*)
4. Longfellow Deeds
5. Elwood P. Dowd (from *Harvey*) ▸

The Best-Known *Shmuck* in the World?
(continued)

Five Famous Fictional *Shmucks*

1. Scarlett O'Hara
2. George Costanza
3. Frasier Crane
4. Mel Cooley (from *The Dick Van Dyke Show*)
5. Dr. McCoy (from *Star Trek*)

We can narrow things down even further, make them a bit more challenging, by making the field of operations smaller. Imagine something like "*Mentshn* and *Shmucks* on *Lost*" or even tougher theoretical questions: "Homer Simpson: *Mentsh* or *Shmuck*?" I don't think there's much arguing about the following, though:

Six *Shmucks* from *The Simpsons*

1. Montgomery Burns
2. Waylon Smithers
3. Lionel Hutz
4. Chief Wiggum
5. Morris "Moe" Szyslak
6. Artie Ziff ∿

Have You Read?
More by Michael Wex

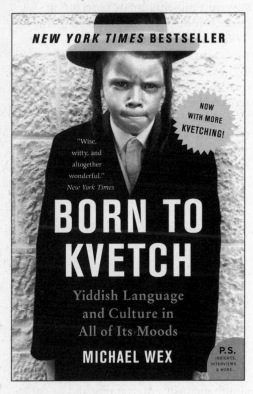

NEW YORK TIMES BESTSELLER

NOW WITH MORE KVETCHING!

"Wise, witty, and altogether wonderful."
New York Times

BORN TO KVETCH

Yiddish Language and Culture in All of Its Moods

MICHAEL WEX

P.S. INSIGHTS, INTERVIEWS & MORE...

BORN TO KVETCH

A delightful excursion through the Yiddish language, the culture it defines and serves, and the fine art of complaint.

Throughout history, Jews around the world have had plenty of reasons to lament. And for a thousand years, they've had the perfect language for it. Rich in color, expressiveness, and complexity, Yiddish has proven incredibly useful and durable. Its wonderful phrases and idioms impeccably reflect the mind-set that has enabled the Jews of Europe to survive a millennium of unrelenting persecution . . . and has enabled them to *kvetch* about it! Michael Wex—professor, scholar, translator, novelist, and performer—takes a serious yet unceasingly fun and funny look at this remarkable, kvetch-ful tongue that has both shaped and has been shaped by those who speak it. Taking on curse words, food, sex, and even death, his lively wit and scholarship roam freely from Sholem Aleichem to Chaucer to Elvis.

"Wise, witty, and altogether wonderful."
—*New York Times*

"Required reading."   —*New York Post*

"[A] treasure trove of linguistics, sociology, history, and folklore."
—*Publishers Weekly* (starred review)

"A work that manages to be simultaneously entertaining and erudite. . . . The results are a joy to behold."   —*Washington Post*

"With verve, élan, and something only a non-Yiddish speaker would call chutzpah, Michael Wex returns to the linguistic mother lode that yielded *Born to Kvetch*.... Mr. Wex, like a Yiddish sommelier, knows just the expression for [any] occasion."
—*NEW YORK TIMES*

JUST SAY NU

Yiddish for Every Occasion
(When English Just Won't Do)

MICHAEL WEX
BESTSELLING AUTHOR OF
BORN TO KVETCH

P.S.
INSIGHTS,
INTERVIEWS
& MORE...

JUST SAY NU

In his *New York Times* bestseller *Born to Kvetch*, author Michael Wex led readers on a hilariously edifying excursion through Yiddish culture and history. With *Just Say Nu*, he shows us how to use this remarkable language to spice up conversations, stories, presentations, arguments, and more, when plain English will not suffice—including, of course, lots of delightful historical and cultural side trips along the way.

There is, quite simply, nothing in the world that can't be improved by being translated into Yiddish. With *Just Say Nu*, readers will learn how to schmooze their way through meeting and greeting, eating and drinking, praising and finding fault, maintaining personal hygiene, parenting, going to the doctor, committing crimes, going to singles bars, having sex, talking politics, talking trash, and a host of other mundane activities. Here also is a healthy schmear of optional grammar and the five most useful Yiddish words—what they mean, and how and when to use them in an entire conversation without anybody suspecting you don't have the vaguest idea about what you're actually saying.

"This is not your bubbe's—or Leo Rosten's—Yiddish. Translator, novelist, and performer Wex follows his witty and erudite *Born to Kvetch* with a colorful, uncensored guide to the idiomatic use of Yiddish in such areas as madness, fury, and driving, and mob Yiddish, insults, and thirteen designations for the human rear—in declining order of politeness."
—*Publishers Weekly*

"When a *tipesh* (moron) dawdles in front of you on the highway, selecting the right curse matters. Mr. Wex, like a Yiddish sommelier, knows just the expression for this or any other occasion."
—William Grimes, *New York Times*

"It just goes to show you the value of Wex's advice: 'Uttered in the proper tone of voice, virtually any phrase in this book can be turned into an insult.'"
—Nora Krug, *Washington Post*